THIS IS YOUR **PASSBOOK**® FOR ...

CONSTRUCTION PROJECT MANAGER

NATIONAL LEARNING CORPORATION®
passbooks.com

PASSBOOK® SERIES

THE *PASSBOOK® SERIES* has been created to prepare applicants and candidates for the ultimate academic battlefield – the examination room.

At some time in our lives, each and every one of us may be required to take an examination – for validation, matriculation, admission, qualification, registration, certification, or licensure.

Based on the assumption that every applicant or candidate has met the basic formal educational standards, has taken the required number of courses, and read the necessary texts, the *PASSBOOK® SERIES* furnishes the one special preparation which may assure passing with confidence, instead of failing with insecurity. Examination questions – together with answers – are furnished as the basic vehicle for study so that the mysteries of the examination and its compounding difficulties may be eliminated or diminished by a sure method.

This book is meant to help you pass your examination provided that you qualify and are serious in your objective.

The entire field is reviewed through the huge store of content information which is succinctly presented through a provocative and challenging approach – the question-and-answer method.

A climate of success is established by furnishing the correct answers at the end of each test.

You soon learn to recognize types of questions, forms of questions, and patterns of questioning. You may even begin to anticipate expected outcomes.

You perceive that many questions are repeated or adapted so that you can gain acute insights, which may enable you to score many sure points.

You learn how to confront new questions, or types of questions, and to attack them confidently and work out the correct answers.

You note objectives and emphases, and recognize pitfalls and dangers, so that you may make positive educational adjustments.

Moreover, you are kept fully informed in relation to new concepts, methods, practices, and directions in the field.

You discover that you arre actually taking the examination all the time: you are preparing for the examination by "taking" an examination, not by reading extraneous and/or supererogatory textbooks.

In short, this PASSBOOK®, used directedly, should be an important factor in helping you to pass your test.

CONSTRUCTION PROJECT MANAGER

DUTIES.

This is a supervisory technical class of positions with varying degrees of difficulty and responsibility encompassing construction project management work and the oversight of construction work necessary for constructing, rehabilitating, renovating and maintaining public buildings, structures, infrastructures, facilities and grounds or publicly owned, subsidized or regulated residential buildings.

At Assignment Level I: Construction Project Managers, under general supervision, perform construction management work and/or initiate and supervise work in the construction field including overseeing rehabilitation projects, or assisting in overseeing routine reconstruction projects; perform difficult technical work in determining the need for and feasibility of construction work; oversee private contractors/vendors carrying out new construction, rehabilitation, repairs, alterations and/or structural maintenance work. They inspect buildings, structures and grounds at regular intervals to ascertain rehabilitation/maintenance needs with regard to construction, equipment and materials; determine the work required and method(s) to be utilized; recommend priorities; monitor work in progress by staff and/or by contractors; report all hazardous conditions; in the Department of Housing Preservation and Development authorize the issuance of repair jobs to vendors; identify problems in construction and seek their resolution; prepare shop orders, scope of work, routine specifications and cost estimates; monitor contractors' day to day operations; review and/or inspect contractors' work and contract administration for compliance with plans and contract specifications, prevailing wage requirements, site safety requirements, insurance requirements, and the City's vendor outreach programs; ensure contractors' acquisition of required permits and approvals; accept contractors' submissions of subcontractors for approval and ensure agency's review; formally evaluate performance of contractors, reporting on discrepancies and/or unsatisfactory performance; when appropriate, issue field memoranda to contractors to enforce contract compliance issues; may order contractors to stop work due to site conditions or non-compliance with contracts; make recommendations regarding necessity for liquidated damages and other contract enforcement mechanisms, including default; ensure the formulation of punch lists and contractors' completion of punch list items; monitor time expenditures and overtime; review and recommend approval of contractors' requests for time extensions; review for approval materials used by contractor; approve contractors' coordination of schedules, and/or coordinate scheduling; coordinate work of various contractors, trades, agencies and entities to expedite the work and minimize interference with the building's functioning; schedule and run job meetings; resolve differences between inspectors and contractors/vendors; work with the architect or engineer of record regarding change orders, interpretation of documents, shop drawing approvals, and other architectural and engineering related issues; recommend issuance of change orders to comply with changing field conditions or specification/drawing errors and/or omissions; upon approval of recommendation, prepare change orders; review and approve other contract changes in accordance with citywide procedures; review and approve contractors' payments and requisitions submitted by contractors; maintain contract files and written records of job history, type, responsibility and progress; use computer to maintain files and to generate reports, correspondence and other paperwork; investigate and advise the agency concerning contract disputes, and appeals on rejection of equipment, materials or workmanship; compile contract and project documentation bearing on these dispute claims; act as liaison with the community and members of the public; prepare reports and correspondence for approval in dealings with contractors and the public, etc.; in the event of any unlawful activity on the construction site, act as the City's representatives in the filing of complaints with the

Police Department or other agencies; provide technical assistance to property managers; operate a motor vehicle to visit job sites; may oversee the work of consultant resident engineers and construction managers; and of consultant design personnel providing construction support services; may supervise staff performing asbestos removal or lead abatement work involving removal or encapsulation of lead contained in or on any surface. All Construction Project Managers perform related work.

THE TEST:
The multiple-choice test may include questions on construction techniques, materials, equipment and safety practices; pertinent parts of the Building and other applicable codes and laws; contracts, plans, specifications, payments, and change orders; scheduling and coordination of work; job-related mathematics; report writing; record keeping; and other related areas.

HOW TO TAKE A TEST

I. YOU MUST PASS AN EXAMINATION

A. *WHAT EVERY CANDIDATE SHOULD KNOW*

Examination applicants often ask us for help in preparing for the written test. What can I study in advance? What kinds of questions will be asked? How will the test be given? How will the papers be graded?

As an applicant for a civil service examination, you may be wondering about some of these things. Our purpose here is to suggest effective methods of advance study and to describe civil service examinations.

Your chances for success on this examination can be increased if you know how to prepare. Those "pre-examination jitters" can be reduced if you know what to expect. You can even experience an adventure in good citizenship if you know why civil service exams are given.

B. *WHY ARE CIVIL SERVICE EXAMINATIONS GIVEN?*

Civil service examinations are important to you in two ways. As a citizen, you want public jobs filled by employees who know how to do their work. As a job seeker, you want a fair chance to compete for that job on an equal footing with other candidates. The best-known means of accomplishing this two-fold goal is the competitive examination.

Exams are widely publicized throughout the nation. They may be administered for jobs in federal, state, city, municipal, town or village governments or agencies.

Any citizen may apply, with some limitations, such as the age or residence of applicants. Your experience and education may be reviewed to see whether you meet the requirements for the particular examination. When these requirements exist, they are reasonable and applied consistently to all applicants. Thus, a competitive examination may cause you some uneasiness now, but it is your privilege and safeguard.

C. *HOW ARE CIVIL SERVICE EXAMS DEVELOPED?*

Examinations are carefully written by trained technicians who are specialists in the field known as "psychological measurement," in consultation with recognized authorities in the field of work that the test will cover. These experts recommend the subject matter areas or skills to be tested; only those knowledges or skills important to your success on the job are included. The most reliable books and source materials available are used as references. Together, the experts and technicians judge the difficulty level of the questions.

Test technicians know how to phrase questions so that the problem is clearly stated. Their ethics do not permit "trick" or "catch" questions. Questions may have been tried out on sample groups, or subjected to statistical analysis, to determine their usefulness.

Written tests are often used in combination with performance tests, ratings of training and experience, and oral interviews. All of these measures combine to form the best-known means of finding the right person for the right job.

II. HOW TO PASS THE WRITTEN TEST

A. NATURE OF THE EXAMINATION

To prepare intelligently for civil service examinations, you should know how they differ from school examinations you have taken. In school you were assigned certain definite pages to read or subjects to cover. The examination questions were quite detailed and usually emphasized memory. Civil service exams, on the other hand, try to discover your present ability to perform the duties of a position, plus your potentiality to learn these duties. In other words, a civil service exam attempts to predict how successful you will be. Questions cover such a broad area that they cannot be as minute and detailed as school exam questions.

In the public service similar kinds of work, or positions, are grouped together in one "class." This process is known as *position-classification*. All the positions in a class are paid according to the salary range for that class. One class title covers all of these positions, and they are all tested by the same examination.

B. FOUR BASIC STEPS

1) Study the announcement

How, then, can you know what subjects to study? Our best answer is: "Learn as much as possible about the class of positions for which you've applied." The exam will test the knowledge, skills and abilities needed to do the work.

Your most valuable source of information about the position you want is the official exam announcement. This announcement lists the training and experience qualifications. Check these standards and apply only if you come reasonably close to meeting them.

The brief description of the position in the examination announcement offers some clues to the subjects which will be tested. Think about the job itself. Review the duties in your mind. Can you perform them, or are there some in which you are rusty? Fill in the blank spots in your preparation.

Many jurisdictions preview the written test in the exam announcement by including a section called "Knowledge and Abilities Required," "Scope of the Examination," or some similar heading. Here you will find out specifically what fields will be tested.

2) Review your own background

Once you learn in general what the position is all about, and what you need to know to do the work, ask yourself which subjects you already know fairly well and which need improvement. You may wonder whether to concentrate on improving your strong areas or on building some background in your fields of weakness. When the announcement has specified "some knowledge" or "considerable knowledge," or has used adjectives like "beginning principles of…" or "advanced … methods," you can get a clue as to the number and difficulty of questions to be asked in any given field. More questions, and hence broader coverage, would be included for those subjects which are more important in the work. Now weigh your strengths and weaknesses against the job requirements and prepare accordingly.

3) Determine the level of the position

Another way to tell how intensively you should prepare is to understand the level of the job for which you are applying. Is it the entering level? In other words, is this the position in which beginners in a field of work are hired? Or is it an intermediate or advanced level? Sometimes this is indicated by such words as "Junior" or "Senior" in the class title. Other jurisdictions use Roman numerals to designate the level – Clerk I, Clerk II, for example. The word "Supervisor" sometimes appears in the title. If the level is not indicated by the title, check the description of duties. Will you be working under very close supervision, or will you have responsibility for independent decisions in this work?

4) Choose appropriate study materials

Now that you know the subjects to be examined and the relative amount of each subject to be covered, you can choose suitable study materials. For beginning level jobs, or even advanced ones, if you have a pronounced weakness in some aspect of your training, read a modern, standard textbook in that field. Be sure it is up to date and has general coverage. Such books are normally available at your library, and the librarian will be glad to help you locate one. For entry-level positions, questions of appropriate difficulty are chosen – neither highly advanced questions, nor those too simple. Such questions require careful thought but not advanced training.

If the position for which you are applying is technical or advanced, you will read more advanced, specialized material. If you are already familiar with the basic principles of your field, elementary textbooks would waste your time. Concentrate on advanced textbooks and technical periodicals. Think through the concepts and review difficult problems in your field.

These are all general sources. You can get more ideas on your own initiative, following these leads. For example, training manuals and publications of the government agency which employs workers in your field can be useful, particularly for technical and professional positions. A letter or visit to the government department involved may result in more specific study suggestions, and certainly will provide you with a more definite idea of the exact nature of the position you are seeking.

III. KINDS OF TESTS

Tests are used for purposes other than measuring knowledge and ability to perform specified duties. For some positions, it is equally important to test ability to make adjustments to new situations or to profit from training. In others, basic mental abilities not dependent on information are essential. Questions which test these things may not appear as pertinent to the duties of the position as those which test for knowledge and information. Yet they are often highly important parts of a fair examination. For very general questions, it is almost impossible to help you direct your study efforts. What we can do is to point out some of the more common of these general abilities needed in public service positions and describe some typical questions.

1) General information

Broad, general information has been found useful for predicting job success in some kinds of work. This is tested in a variety of ways, from vocabulary lists to questions about current events. Basic background in some field of work, such as sociology or economics, may be sampled in a group of questions. Often these are principles which have become familiar to most persons through exposure rather than through formal training. It is difficult to advise you how to study for these questions; being alert to the world around you is our best suggestion.

2) Verbal ability

An example of an ability needed in many positions is verbal or language ability. Verbal ability is, in brief, the ability to use and understand words. Vocabulary and grammar tests are typical measures of this ability. Reading comprehension or paragraph interpretation questions are common in many kinds of civil service tests. You are given a paragraph of written material and asked to find its central meaning.

3) Numerical ability

Number skills can be tested by the familiar arithmetic problem, by checking paired lists of numbers to see which are alike and which are different, or by interpreting charts and graphs. In the latter test, a graph may be printed in the test booklet which you are asked to use as the basis for answering questions.

4) Observation

A popular test for law-enforcement positions is the observation test. A picture is shown to you for several minutes, then taken away. Questions about the picture test your ability to observe both details and larger elements.

5) Following directions

In many positions in the public service, the employee must be able to carry out written instructions dependably and accurately. You may be given a chart with several columns, each column listing a variety of information. The questions require you to carry out directions involving the information given in the chart.

6) Skills and aptitudes

Performance tests effectively measure some manual skills and aptitudes. When the skill is one in which you are trained, such as typing or shorthand, you can practice. These tests are often very much like those given in business school or high school courses. For many of the other skills and aptitudes, however, no short-time preparation can be made. Skills and abilities natural to you or that you have developed throughout your lifetime are being tested.

Many of the general questions just described provide all the data needed to answer the questions and ask you to use your reasoning ability to find the answers. Your best preparation for these tests, as well as for tests of facts and ideas, is to be at your physical and mental best. You, no doubt, have your own methods of getting into an exam-taking mood and keeping "in shape." The next section lists some ideas on this subject.

IV. KINDS OF QUESTIONS

Only rarely is the "essay" question, which you answer in narrative form, used in civil service tests. Civil service tests are usually of the short-answer type. Full instructions for answering these questions will be given to you at the examination. But in case this is your first experience with short-answer questions and separate answer sheets, here is what you need to know:

1) Multiple-choice Questions

Most popular of the short-answer questions is the "multiple choice" or "best answer" question. It can be used, for example, to test for factual knowledge, ability to solve problems or judgment in meeting situations found at work.

A multiple-choice question is normally one of three types—
- It can begin with an incomplete statement followed by several possible endings. You are to find the one ending which *best* completes the statement, although some of the others may not be entirely wrong.
- It can also be a complete statement in the form of a question which is answered by choosing one of the statements listed.
- It can be in the form of a problem – again you select the best answer.

Here is an example of a multiple-choice question with a discussion which should give you some clues as to the method for choosing the right answer:

When an employee has a complaint about his assignment, the action which will *best* help him overcome his difficulty is to
- A. discuss his difficulty with his coworkers
- B. take the problem to the head of the organization
- C. take the problem to the person who gave him the assignment
- D. say nothing to anyone about his complaint

In answering this question, you should study each of the choices to find which is best. Consider choice "A" – Certainly an employee may discuss his complaint with fellow employees, but no change or improvement can result, and the complaint remains unresolved. Choice "B" is a poor choice since the head of the organization probably does not know what assignment you have been given, and taking your problem to him is known as "going over the head" of the supervisor. The supervisor, or person who made the assignment, is the person who can clarify it or correct any injustice. Choice "C" is, therefore, correct. To say nothing, as in choice "D," is unwise. Supervisors have and interest in knowing the problems employees are facing, and the employee is seeking a solution to his problem.

2) True/False Questions

The "true/false" or "right/wrong" form of question is sometimes used. Here a complete statement is given. Your job is to decide whether the statement is right or wrong.

SAMPLE: A roaming cell-phone call to a nearby city costs less than a non-roaming call to a distant city.

This statement is wrong, or false, since roaming calls are more expensive.
This is not a complete list of all possible question forms, although most of the others are variations of these common types. You will always get complete directions for

answering questions. Be sure you understand *how* to mark your answers – ask questions until you do.

V. RECORDING YOUR ANSWERS

Computer terminals are used more and more today for many different kinds of exams.

For an examination with very few applicants, you may be told to record your answers in the test booklet itself. Separate answer sheets are much more common. If this separate answer sheet is to be scored by machine – and this is often the case – it is highly important that you mark your answers correctly in order to get credit.

An electronic scoring machine is often used in civil service offices because of the speed with which papers can be scored. Machine-scored answer sheets must be marked with a pencil, which will be given to you. This pencil has a high graphite content which responds to the electronic scoring machine. As a matter of fact, stray dots may register as answers, so do not let your pencil rest on the answer sheet while you are pondering the correct answer. Also, if your pencil lead breaks or is otherwise defective, ask for another.

Since the answer sheet will be dropped in a slot in the scoring machine, be careful not to bend the corners or get the paper crumpled.

The answer sheet normally has five vertical columns of numbers, with 30 numbers to a column. These numbers correspond to the question numbers in your test booklet. After each number, going across the page are four or five pairs of dotted lines. These short dotted lines have small letters or numbers above them. The first two pairs may also have a "T" or "F" above the letters. This indicates that the first two pairs only are to be used if the questions are of the true-false type. If the questions are multiple choice, disregard the "T" and "F" and pay attention only to the small letters or numbers.

Answer your questions in the manner of the sample that follows:

32. The largest city in the United States is
      A. Washington, D.C.
      B. New York City
      C. Chicago
      D. Detroit
      E. San Francisco

1) Choose the answer you think is best. (New York City is the largest, so "B" is correct.)
2) Find the row of dotted lines numbered the same as the question you are answering. (Find row number 32)
3) Find the pair of dotted lines corresponding to the answer. (Find the pair of lines under the mark "B.")
4) Make a solid black mark between the dotted lines.

VI. BEFORE THE TEST

Common sense will help you find procedures to follow to get ready for an examination. Too many of us, however, overlook these sensible measures. Indeed, nervousness and fatigue have been found to be the most serious reasons why applicants fail to do their best on civil service tests. Here is a list of reminders:

- Begin your preparation early – Don't wait until the last minute to go scurrying around for books and materials or to find out what the position is all about.
- Prepare continuously – An hour a night for a week is better than an all-night cram session. This has been definitely established. What is more, a night a week for a month will return better dividends than crowding your study into a shorter period of time.
- Locate the place of the exam – You have been sent a notice telling you when and where to report for the examination. If the location is in a different town or otherwise unfamiliar to you, it would be well to inquire the best route and learn something about the building.
- Relax the night before the test – Allow your mind to rest. Do not study at all that night. Plan some mild recreation or diversion; then go to bed early and get a good night's sleep.
- Get up early enough to make a leisurely trip to the place for the test – This way unforeseen events, traffic snarls, unfamiliar buildings, etc. will not upset you.
- Dress comfortably – A written test is not a fashion show. You will be known by number and not by name, so wear something comfortable.
- Leave excess paraphernalia at home – Shopping bags and odd bundles will get in your way. You need bring only the items mentioned in the official notice you received; usually everything you need is provided. Do not bring reference books to the exam. They will only confuse those last minutes and be taken away from you when in the test room.
- Arrive somewhat ahead of time – If because of transportation schedules you must get there very early, bring a newspaper or magazine to take your mind off yourself while waiting.
- Locate the examination room – When you have found the proper room, you will be directed to the seat or part of the room where you will sit. Sometimes you are given a sheet of instructions to read while you are waiting. Do not fill out any forms until you are told to do so; just read them and be prepared.
- Relax and prepare to listen to the instructions
- If you have any physical problem that may keep you from doing your best, be sure to tell the test administrator. If you are sick or in poor health, you really cannot do your best on the exam. You can come back and take the test some other time.

VII. AT THE TEST

The day of the test is here and you have the test booklet in your hand. The temptation to get going is very strong. Caution! There is more to success than knowing the right answers. You must know how to identify your papers and understand variations in the type of short-answer question used in this particular examination. Follow these suggestions for maximum results from your efforts:

1) Cooperate with the monitor

The test administrator has a duty to create a situation in which you can be as much at ease as possible. He will give instructions, tell you when to begin, check to see that you are marking your answer sheet correctly, and so on. He is not there to guard you, although he will see that your competitors do not take unfair advantage. He wants to help you do your best.

2) Listen to all instructions

Don't jump the gun! Wait until you understand all directions. In most civil service tests you get more time than you need to answer the questions. So don't be in a hurry. Read each word of instructions until you clearly understand the meaning. Study the examples, listen to all announcements and follow directions. Ask questions if you do not understand what to do.

3) Identify your papers

Civil service exams are usually identified by number only. You will be assigned a number; you must not put your name on your test papers. Be sure to copy your number correctly. Since more than one exam may be given, copy your exact examination title.

4) Plan your time

Unless you are told that a test is a "speed" or "rate of work" test, speed itself is usually not important. Time enough to answer all the questions will be provided, but this does not mean that you have all day. An overall time limit has been set. Divide the total time (in minutes) by the number of questions to determine the approximate time you have for each question.

5) Do not linger over difficult questions

If you come across a difficult question, mark it with a paper clip (useful to have along) and come back to it when you have been through the booklet. One caution if you do this – be sure to skip a number on your answer sheet as well. Check often to be sure that you have not lost your place and that you are marking in the row numbered the same as the question you are answering.

6) Read the questions

Be sure you know what the question asks! Many capable people are unsuccessful because they failed to *read* the questions correctly.

7) Answer all questions

Unless you have been instructed that a penalty will be deducted for incorrect answers, it is better to guess than to omit a question.

8) Speed tests

It is often better NOT to guess on speed tests. It has been found that on timed tests people are tempted to spend the last few seconds before time is called in marking answers at random – without even reading them – in the hope of picking up a few extra points. To discourage this practice, the instructions may warn you that your score will be "corrected" for guessing. That is, a penalty will be applied. The incorrect answers will be deducted from the correct ones, or some other penalty formula will be used.

9) Review your answers

If you finish before time is called, go back to the questions you guessed or omitted to give them further thought. Review other answers if you have time.

10) Return your test materials

If you are ready to leave before others have finished or time is called, take ALL your materials to the monitor and leave quietly. Never take any test material with you. The monitor can discover whose papers are not complete, and taking a test booklet may be grounds for disqualification.

VIII. EXAMINATION TECHNIQUES

1) Read the general instructions carefully. These are usually printed on the first page of the exam booklet. As a rule, these instructions refer to the timing of the examination; the fact that you should not start work until the signal and must stop work at a signal, etc. If there are any *special* instructions, such as a choice of questions to be answered, make sure that you note this instruction carefully.

2) When you are ready to start work on the examination, that is as soon as the signal has been given, read the instructions to each question booklet, underline any key words or phrases, such as *least, best, outline, describe* and the like. In this way you will tend to answer as requested rather than discover on reviewing your paper that you *listed without describing*, that you selected the *worst* choice rather than the *best* choice, etc.

3) If the examination is of the objective or multiple-choice type – that is, each question will also give a series of possible answers: A, B, C or D, and you are called upon to select the best answer and write the letter next to that answer on your answer paper – it is advisable to start answering each question in turn. There may be anywhere from 50 to 100 such questions in the three or four hours allotted and you can see how much time would be taken if you read through all the questions before beginning to answer any. Furthermore, if you come across a question or group of questions which you know would be difficult to answer, it would undoubtedly affect your handling of all the other questions.

4) If the examination is of the essay type and contains but a few questions, it is a moot point as to whether you should read all the questions before starting to answer any one. Of course, if you are given a choice – say five out of seven and the like – then it is essential to read all the questions so you can eliminate the two that are most difficult. If, however, you are asked to answer all the questions, there may be danger in trying to answer the easiest one first because you may find that you will spend too much time on it. The best technique is to answer the first question, then proceed to the second, etc.

5) Time your answers. Before the exam begins, write down the time it started, then add the time allowed for the examination and write down the time it must be completed, then divide the time available somewhat as follows:

- If 3-1/2 hours are allowed, that would be 210 minutes. If you have 80 objective-type questions, that would be an average of 2-1/2 minutes per question. Allow yourself no more than 2 minutes per question, or a total of 160 minutes, which will permit about 50 minutes to review.
- If for the time allotment of 210 minutes there are 7 essay questions to answer, that would average about 30 minutes a question. Give yourself only 25 minutes per question so that you have about 35 minutes to review.

6) The most important instruction is to *read each question* and make sure you know what is wanted. The second most important instruction is to *time yourself properly* so that you answer every question. The third most important instruction is to *answer every question*. Guess if you have to but include something for each question. Remember that you will receive no credit for a blank and will probably receive some credit if you write something in answer to an essay question. If you guess a letter – say "B" for a multiple-choice question – you may have guessed right. If you leave a blank as an answer to a multiple-choice question, the examiners may respect your feelings but it will not add a point to your score. Some exams may penalize you for wrong answers, so in such cases *only*, you may not want to guess unless you have some basis for your answer.

7) Suggestions
   a. Objective-type questions
      1. Examine the question booklet for proper sequence of pages and questions
      2. Read all instructions carefully
      3. Skip any question which seems too difficult; return to it after all other questions have been answered
      4. Apportion your time properly; do not spend too much time on any single question or group of questions
      5. Note and underline key words – *all, most, fewest, least, best, worst, same, opposite,* etc.
      6. Pay particular attention to negatives
      7. Note unusual option, e.g., unduly long, short, complex, different or similar in content to the body of the question
      8. Observe the use of "hedging" words – *probably, may, most likely,* etc.
      9. Make sure that your answer is put next to the same number as the question
      10. Do not second-guess unless you have good reason to believe the second answer is definitely more correct
      11. Cross out original answer if you decide another answer is more accurate; do not erase until you are ready to hand your paper in
      12. Answer all questions; guess unless instructed otherwise
      13. Leave time for review

   b. Essay questions
      1. Read each question carefully
      2. Determine exactly what is wanted. Underline key words or phrases.
      3. Decide on outline or paragraph answer

4. Include many different points and elements unless asked to develop any one or two points or elements
5. Show impartiality by giving pros and cons unless directed to select one side only
6. Make and write down any assumptions you find necessary to answer the questions
7. Watch your English, grammar, punctuation and choice of words
8. Time your answers; don't crowd material

8) Answering the essay question

Most essay questions can be answered by framing the specific response around several key words or ideas. Here are a few such key words or ideas:

M's: manpower, materials, methods, money, management
P's: purpose, program, policy, plan, procedure, practice, problems, pitfalls, personnel, public relations

a. Six basic steps in handling problems:
   1. Preliminary plan and background development
   2. Collect information, data and facts
   3. Analyze and interpret information, data and facts
   4. Analyze and develop solutions as well as make recommendations
   5. Prepare report and sell recommendations
   6. Install recommendations and follow up effectiveness

b. Pitfalls to avoid
   1. *Taking things for granted* – A statement of the situation does not necessarily imply that each of the elements is necessarily true; for example, a complaint may be invalid and biased so that all that can be taken for granted is that a complaint has been registered
   2. *Considering only one side of a situation* – Wherever possible, indicate several alternatives and then point out the reasons you selected the best one
   3. *Failing to indicate follow up* – Whenever your answer indicates action on your part, make certain that you will take proper follow-up action to see how successful your recommendations, procedures or actions turn out to be
   4. *Taking too long in answering any single question* – Remember to time your answers properly

IX. AFTER THE TEST

Scoring procedures differ in detail among civil service jurisdictions although the general principles are the same. Whether the papers are hand-scored or graded by machine we have described, they are nearly always graded by number. That is, the person who marks the paper knows only the number – never the name – of the applicant. Not until all the papers have been graded will they be matched with names. If other tests, such as training and experience or oral interview ratings have been given, scores will be combined. Different parts of the examination usually have different weights. For example, the written test might count 60 percent of the final grade, and a rating of training and experience 40 percent. In many jurisdictions, veterans will have a certain number of points added to their grades.

After the final grade has been determined, the names are placed in grade order and an eligible list is established. There are various methods for resolving ties between those who get the same final grade – probably the most common is to place first the name of the person whose application was received first. Job offers are made from the eligible list in the order the names appear on it. You will be notified of your grade and your rank as soon as all these computations have been made. This will be done as rapidly as possible.

People who are found to meet the requirements in the announcement are called "eligibles." Their names are put on a list of eligible candidates. An eligible's chances of getting a job depend on how high he stands on this list and how fast agencies are filling jobs from the list.

When a job is to be filled from a list of eligibles, the agency asks for the names of people on the list of eligibles for that job. When the civil service commission receives this request, it sends to the agency the names of the three people highest on this list. Or, if the job to be filled has specialized requirements, the office sends the agency the names of the top three persons who meet these requirements from the general list.

The appointing officer makes a choice from among the three people whose names were sent to him. If the selected person accepts the appointment, the names of the others are put back on the list to be considered for future openings.

That is the rule in hiring from all kinds of eligible lists, whether they are for typist, carpenter, chemist, or something else. For every vacancy, the appointing officer has his choice of any one of the top three eligibles on the list. This explains why the person whose name is on top of the list sometimes does not get an appointment when some of the persons lower on the list do. If the appointing officer chooses the second or third eligible, the No. 1 eligible does not get a job at once, but stays on the list until he is appointed or the list is terminated.

X. HOW TO PASS THE INTERVIEW TEST

The examination for which you applied requires an oral interview test. You have already taken the written test and you are now being called for the interview test – the final part of the formal examination.

You may think that it is not possible to prepare for an interview test and that there are no procedures to follow during an interview. Our purpose is to point out some things you can do in advance that will help you and some good rules to follow and pitfalls to avoid while you are being interviewed.

What is an interview supposed to test?
The written examination is designed to test the technical knowledge and competence of the candidate; the oral is designed to evaluate intangible qualities, not readily measured otherwise, and to establish a list showing the relative fitness of each candidate – as measured against his competitors – for the position sought. Scoring is not on the basis of "right" and "wrong," but on a sliding scale of values ranging from "not passable" to "outstanding." As a matter of fact, it is possible to achieve a relatively low score without a single "incorrect" answer because of evident weakness in the qualities being measured.

Occasionally, an examination may consist entirely of an oral test – either an individual or a group oral. In such cases, information is sought concerning the technical knowledges and abilities of the candidate, since there has been no written examination for this purpose. More commonly, however, an oral test is used to supplement a written examination.

Who conducts interviews?

The composition of oral boards varies among different jurisdictions. In nearly all, a representative of the personnel department serves as chairman. One of the members of the board may be a representative of the department in which the candidate would work. In some cases, "outside experts" are used, and, frequently, a businessman or some other representative of the general public is asked to serve. Labor and management or other special groups may be represented. The aim is to secure the services of experts in the appropriate field.

However the board is composed, it is a good idea (and not at all improper or unethical) to ascertain in advance of the interview who the members are and what groups they represent. When you are introduced to them, you will have some idea of their backgrounds and interests, and at least you will not stutter and stammer over their names.

What should be done before the interview?

While knowledge about the board members is useful and takes some of the surprise element out of the interview, there is other preparation which is more substantive. It *is* possible to prepare for an oral interview – in several ways:

1) Keep a copy of your application and review it carefully before the interview

This may be the only document before the oral board, and the starting point of the interview. Know what education and experience you have listed there, and the sequence and dates of all of it. Sometimes the board will ask you to review the highlights of your experience for them; you should not have to hem and haw doing it.

2) Study the class specification and the examination announcement

Usually, the oral board has one or both of these to guide them. The qualities, characteristics or knowledges required by the position sought are stated in these documents. They offer valuable clues as to the nature of the oral interview. For example, if the job involves supervisory responsibilities, the announcement will usually indicate that knowledge of modern supervisory methods and the qualifications of the candidate as a supervisor will be tested. If so, you can expect such questions, frequently in the form of a hypothetical situation which you are expected to solve. NEVER go into an oral without knowledge of the duties and responsibilities of the job you seek.

3) Think through each qualification required

Try to visualize the kind of questions you would ask if you were a board member. How well could you answer them? Try especially to appraise your own knowledge and background in each area, *measured against the job sought*, and identify any areas in which you are weak. Be critical and realistic – do not flatter yourself.

4) Do some general reading in areas in which you feel you may be weak

For example, if the job involves supervision and your past experience has NOT, some general reading in supervisory methods and practices, particularly in the field of human relations, might be useful. Do NOT study agency procedures or detailed manuals. The oral board will be testing your understanding and capacity, not your memory.

5) Get a good night's sleep and watch your general health and mental attitude

You will want a clear head at the interview. Take care of a cold or any other minor ailment, and of course, no hangovers.

What should be done on the day of the interview?

Now comes the day of the interview itself. Give yourself plenty of time to get there. Plan to arrive somewhat ahead of the scheduled time, particularly if your appointment is in the fore part of the day. If a previous candidate fails to appear, the board might be ready for you a bit early. By early afternoon an oral board is almost invariably behind schedule if there are many candidates, and you may have to wait. Take along a book or magazine to read, or your application to review, but leave any extraneous material in the waiting room when you go in for your interview. In any event, relax and compose yourself.

The matter of dress is important. The board is forming impressions about you – from your experience, your manners, your attitude, and your appearance. Give your personal appearance careful attention. Dress your best, but not your flashiest. Choose conservative, appropriate clothing, and be sure it is immaculate. This is a business interview, and your appearance should indicate that you regard it as such. Besides, being well groomed and properly dressed will help boost your confidence.

Sooner or later, someone will call your name and escort you into the interview room. *This is it.* From here on you are on your own. It is too late for any more preparation. But remember, you asked for this opportunity to prove your fitness, and you are here because your request was granted.

What happens when you go in?

The usual sequence of events will be as follows: The clerk (who is often the board stenographer) will introduce you to the chairman of the oral board, who will introduce you to the other members of the board. Acknowledge the introductions before you sit down. Do not be surprised if you find a microphone facing you or a stenotypist sitting by. Oral interviews are usually recorded in the event of an appeal or other review.

Usually the chairman of the board will open the interview by reviewing the highlights of your education and work experience from your application – primarily for the benefit of the other members of the board, as well as to get the material into the record. Do not interrupt or comment unless there is an error or significant misinterpretation; if that is the case, do not hesitate. But do not quibble about insignificant matters. Also, he will usually ask you some question about your education, experience or your present job – partly to get you to start talking and to establish the interviewing "rapport." He may start the actual questioning, or turn it over to one of the other members. Frequently, each member undertakes the questioning on a particular area, one in which he is perhaps most competent, so you can expect each member to participate in the examination. Because time is limited, you may also expect some rather abrupt switches in the direction the questioning takes, so do not be upset by it. Normally, a board member will not pursue a single line of questioning unless he discovers a particular strength or weakness.

After each member has participated, the chairman will usually ask whether any member has any further questions, then will ask you if you have anything you wish to add. Unless you are expecting this question, it may floor you. Worse, it may start you off on an extended, extemporaneous speech. The board is not usually seeking more information. The question is principally to offer you a last opportunity to present further qualifications or to indicate that you have nothing to add. So, if you feel that a significant qualification or characteristic has been overlooked, it is proper to point it out in a sentence or so. Do not compliment the board on the thoroughness of their examination – they have been sketchy, and you know it. If you wish, merely say, "No thank you, I have nothing further to add." This is a point where you can "talk yourself out" of a good impression or fail to present an important bit of information. Remember, *you close the interview yourself.*

The chairman will then say, "That is all, Mr. _____, thank you." Do not be startled; the interview is over, and quicker than you think. Thank him, gather your belongings and take your leave. Save your sigh of relief for the other side of the door.

How to put your best foot forward

Throughout this entire process, you may feel that the board individually and collectively is trying to pierce your defenses, seek out your hidden weaknesses and embarrass and confuse you. Actually, this is not true. They are obliged to make an appraisal of your qualifications for the job you are seeking, and they want to see you in your best light. Remember, they must interview all candidates and a non-cooperative candidate may become a failure in spite of their best efforts to bring out his qualifications. Here are 15 suggestions that will help you:

1) Be natural – Keep your attitude confident, not cocky

If you are not confident that you can do the job, do not expect the board to be. Do not apologize for your weaknesses, try to bring out your strong points. The board is interested in a positive, not negative, presentation. Cockiness will antagonize any board member and make him wonder if you are covering up a weakness by a false show of strength.

2) Get comfortable, but don't lounge or sprawl

Sit erectly but not stiffly. A careless posture may lead the board to conclude that you are careless in other things, or at least that you are not impressed by the importance of the occasion. Either conclusion is natural, even if incorrect. Do not fuss with your clothing, a pencil or an ashtray. Your hands may occasionally be useful to emphasize a point; do not let them become a point of distraction.

3) Do not wisecrack or make small talk

This is a serious situation, and your attitude should show that you consider it as such. Further, the time of the board is limited – they do not want to waste it, and neither should you.

4) Do not exaggerate your experience or abilities

In the first place, from information in the application or other interviews and sources, the board may know more about you than you think. Secondly, you probably will not get away with it. An experienced board is rather adept at spotting such a situation, so do not take the chance.

5) If you know a board member, do not make a point of it, yet do not hide it

Certainly you are not fooling him, and probably not the other members of the board. Do not try to take advantage of your acquaintanceship – it will probably do you little good.

6) Do not dominate the interview

Let the board do that. They will give you the clues – do not assume that you have to do all the talking. Realize that the board has a number of questions to ask you, and do not try to take up all the interview time by showing off your extensive knowledge of the answer to the first one.

7) Be attentive

You only have 20 minutes or so, and you should keep your attention at its sharpest throughout. When a member is addressing a problem or question to you, give him your undivided attention. Address your reply principally to him, but do not exclude the other board members.

8) Do not interrupt

A board member may be stating a problem for you to analyze. He will ask you a question when the time comes. Let him state the problem, and wait for the question.

9) Make sure you understand the question

Do not try to answer until you are sure what the question is. If it is not clear, restate it in your own words or ask the board member to clarify it for you. However, do not haggle about minor elements.

10) Reply promptly but not hastily

A common entry on oral board rating sheets is "candidate responded readily," or "candidate hesitated in replies." Respond as promptly and quickly as you can, but do not jump to a hasty, ill-considered answer.

11) Do not be peremptory in your answers

A brief answer is proper – but do not fire your answer back. That is a losing game from your point of view. The board member can probably ask questions much faster than you can answer them.

12) Do not try to create the answer you think the board member wants

He is interested in what kind of mind you have and how it works – not in playing games. Furthermore, he can usually spot this practice and will actually grade you down on it.

13) Do not switch sides in your reply merely to agree with a board member

Frequently, a member will take a contrary position merely to draw you out and to see if you are willing and able to defend your point of view. Do not start a debate, yet do not surrender a good position. If a position is worth taking, it is worth defending.

14) Do not be afraid to admit an error in judgment if you are shown to be wrong

      The board knows that you are forced to reply without any opportunity for careful consideration. Your answer may be demonstrably wrong. If so, admit it and get on with the interview.

15) Do not dwell at length on your present job

      The opening question may relate to your present assignment. Answer the question but do not go into an extended discussion. You are being examined for a *new* job, not your present one. As a matter of fact, try to phrase ALL your answers in terms of the job for which you are being examined.

Basis of Rating

      Probably you will forget most of these "do's" and "don'ts" when you walk into the oral interview room. Even remembering them all will not ensure you a passing grade. Perhaps you did not have the qualifications in the first place. But remembering them will help you to put your best foot forward, without treading on the toes of the board members.

      Rumor and popular opinion to the contrary notwithstanding, an oral board wants you to make the best appearance possible. They know you are under pressure – but they also want to see how you respond to it as a guide to what your reaction would be under the pressures of the job you seek. They will be influenced by the degree of poise you display, the personal traits you show and the manner in which you respond.

ABOUT THIS BOOK

      This book contains tests divided into Examination Sections. Go through each test, answering every question in the margin. At the end of each test look at the answer key and check your answers. On the ones you got wrong, look at the right answer choice and learn. Do not fill in the answers first. Do not memorize the questions and answers, but understand the answer and principles involved. On your test, the questions will likely be different from the samples. Questions are changed and new ones added. If you understand these past questions you should have success with any changes that arise. Tests may consist of several types of questions. We have additional books on each subject should more study be advisable or necessary for you. Finally, the more you study, the better prepared you will be. This book is intended to be the last thing you study before you walk into the examination room. Prior study of relevant texts is also recommended. NLC publishes some of these in our Fundamental Series. Knowledge and good sense are important factors in passing your exam. Good luck also helps. So now study this Passbook, absorb the material contained within and take that knowledge into the examination. Then do your best to pass that exam.

––––––

EXAMINATION SECTION

EXAMINATION SECTION
TEST 1

DIRECTIONS: Each question or incomplete statement is followed by several suggested answers or completions. Select the one that BEST answers the question or completes the statement. *PRINT THE LETTER OF THE CORRECT ANSWER IN THE SPACE AT THE RIGHT.*

1. Management by exception (MBE) is   1.____

    A. designed to locate bottlenecks
    B. designed to pinpoint superior performance
    C. a form of index locating
    D. a form of variance reporting

2. In managerial terms, gap analysis is useful primarily in   2.____

    A. problem solving   B. setting standards
    C. inventory control   D. locating bottlenecks

3. ABC analysis involves   3.____

    A. problem solving   B. indexing
    C. brainstorming   D. inventory control

4. The Federal Discrimination in Employment Act as amended in 1978 prohibits job discrim-   4.____
ination based on age for persons between the ages of

    A. 35 and 60   B. 40 and 65   C. 45 and 65   D. 40 and 70

5. Inspectors should be familiar with the contractor's CPM charts for a construction job pri-   5.____
marily to determine if

    A. the job is on schedule
    B. the contractor is using the charts correctly
    C. material is on hand to keep the job on schedule
    D. there is a potential source of delay

6. The value engineering approach is frequently found in public works contracts. Value   6.____
engineering is

    A. an effort to cut down or eliminate extra work payments
    B. a team approach to optimize the cost of the project
    C. to insure that material and equipment will perform as specified
    D. to insure that insurance costs on the project can be minimized

7. Historically, most costly claims have been either for   7.____

    A. unreasonable inspection requirements or unforeseen weather conditions
    B. unreasonable specification requirements or unreasonable completion time for the contract
    C. added costs due to inflation or unavailability of material
    D. delays or alleged changed conditions

8. A claim is a

    A. dispute that cannot be resolved
    B. dispute arising from ambiguity in the specifications
    C. dispute arising from the quality of the work
    D. recognition that the courts are the sole arbiters of a dispute

8.____

9. Disputes arising between a contractor and the owning agency are

    A. the result of inflexibility of either or both parties to the dispute
    B. mainly the result of shortcomings in the design
    C. the result of shortcomings in the specifications
    D. inevitable

9.____

Questions 10-13.

DIRECTIONS: Questions 10 through 13, inclusive, refers to the array of numbers listed below.

    16, 7, 9, 5, 10, 8, 5, 1, 2

10. The mean of the numbers is

    A. 2   B. 5   C. 7   D. 8

10.____

11. The median of the numbers is

    A. 2   B. 5   C. 7   D. 8

11.____

12. The mode of the numbers is

    A. 2   B. 5   C. 7   D. 8

12.____

13. In statistical measurements, a subgroup that is representative of the entire group is a

    A. commutative group   B. sample
    C. central index   D. Abelian group

13.____

14. Productivity is the ratio of

    A. $\dfrac{\text{product costs}}{\text{labor costs}}$

    B. $\dfrac{\text{cost of final product}}{\text{cost of materials}}$

    C. $\dfrac{\text{outputs}}{\text{inputs}}$

    D. $\dfrac{\text{outputs cost}}{\text{time needed to product the output}}$

14.____

15. Downtime is the time a piece of equipment is

    A. idle waiting for other equipment to become available
    B. not being used for the purpose it was intended

15.____

C. being used inefficiently
D. unavailable for use

16. Index numbers 16.____

    A. relates to the cost of a product as material costs vary
    B. allows the user to find the variation from the norm
    C. are a way of comparing costs of different approaches to a problem
    D. a way of measuring and comparing changes over a period of time

17. The underlying idea behind Management by Objectives is to provide a mechanism for 17.____
managers to

    A. coordinate personal and departmental plans with organizational goals
    B. motivate employees by having them participate in job decisions
    C. motivate employees by training them for the next higher position
    D. set objectives that are reasonable for the employees to attain, thus improving self-esteem among the employees

18. The ultimate objective of the project manager in planning and scheduling a project is to 18.____

    A. meet the completion dates of the project
    B. use the least amount of labor on the project
    C. use the least amount of material on the project
    D. prevent interference between the different trades

19. Scheduling with respect to the critical path method usually does not involve 19.____

    A. cost allocation
    B. starting and finishing time
    C. float for each activity
    D. project duration

20. When CPM is used on a construction project, updates are most commonly made 20.____

    A. weekly   B. every two weeks
    C. monthly   D. every two months

Questions 21-24.

DIRECTIONS: Questions 21 through 24 refer to the following network.

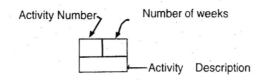

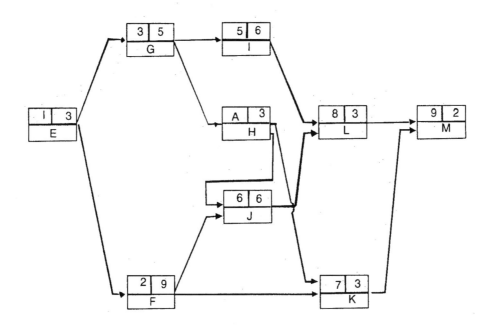

Activity Number	Activity Description	Duration in Weeks	Early Start	Early Finish	Late Start	Late Finish	Total Slack
1	E	3					
2	F	9					
3	G	5					
4	H	3					
5	I	6					
6	J	6					
7	K	3					
8	L	3					
9	M	2					

21. The critical path is

    A. E G H J L M   B. E G I L M
    C. E F J L M   D. E G H K M

21.____

22. The minimum time needed to complete the job is, in weeks,

    A. 19   B. 21   C. 22   D. 23

22.____

23. The slack time in J is, in weeks,

    A. 0   B. 1   C. 2   D. 3

23.____

24. The slack time in K is, in weeks,

    A. 4   B. 5   C. 6   D. 7

24.____

25. Of the following, the primary objective of CPM is to   25.____

    A.   eliminate duplication of work
    B.   overcome obstacles such as bad weather
    C.   spot potential bottlenecks
    D.   save on the cost of material

KEY (CORRECT ANSWERS)

1.	D	11.	C
2.	A	12.	B
3.	D	13.	B
4.	D	14.	C
5.	A	15.	D
6.	B	16.	D
7.	D	17.	A
8.	A	18.	A
9.	D	19.	A
10.	C	20.	C

21.	C
22.	D
23.	A
24.	C
25.	C

TEST 2

Each question or incomplete statement is followed by several suggested answers or completions. Select the one that BEST answers the question or completes the statement. *PRINT THE LETTER OF THE CORRECT ANSWER IN THE SPACE AT THE RIGHT.*

1. Gantt refers to   1.____

    A. bar charts   B. milestone charts
    C. PERT networks   D. Management by Objectives

2. PERT is an abbreviation for   2.____

    A. Progress Evaluation in Real Time
    B. Preliminary Evaluation of Running Time
    C. Program Evaluation Review Techniques
    D. Program Estimation and Repair Times

3. In project management terms, slack is equivalent to   3.____

    A. tare   B. off time   C. delay   D. float

4. The FIRST step in planning and programming a roadway pavement management system   4.____
   is to evaluate

    A. priorities for the work to be done
    B. the condition of your equipment
    C. the condition of the roads in the system
    D. the storage and maintenance facilities

5. Managers accomplish their work in an ever changing environment by integrating three   5.____
   time-tested approaches. The one of the following that is NOT a time-tested approach is

    A. scientific adaptation   B. scientific management
    C. behavior management   D. management sciences

6. The most effective managers manage for optimum results. This means that the manager   6.____
   is seeking to _____ a given situation.

    A. get the maximum results from
    B. get the most favorable results from
    C. get the most reasonable results from
    D. satisfy the conflicting interests in

7. If a manager believes that an employee is irresponsible, the employee, in subtle   7.____
   response to the manager's assessment, will in fact prove to be irresponsible. This is an
   example of a(n)

    A. conditioned reflex   B. self-fulfilling prophesy
    C. Freudian response   D. automatic reaction

8. Perhaps nothing distinguishes the younger generation from the older so much as the   8.____
   value placed on work. The older generation was generally raised to believe in the Protes-
   tant work ethic.
   This ethic holds primarily that

A. people should try to get the highest salary possible
B. work should help people to advance
C. work should be well done if it is interesting
D. work is valuable in itself and the person who does it focuses on his work

9. The standard method currently in use in inspecting bituminous paving is to inspect each activity in detail as the paving work is being installed. In recent years some agencies use a different method of inspection known as a(n)   9.____

A. as-built quality control method
B. statistically controlled quality assurance method
C. data based history of previous contracts of this type
D. performance evaluation of the completed paving contract

10. Aggregates for use in bituminous pavements should be tested for grading,   10.____

A. abrasion, soundness, and specific gravity
B. type of rock, abrasion, and specific gravity
C. abrasion, soundness, and deleterious material
D. specific gravity, chemical composition of the aggregate, and deleterious material

11. Of the following, the one that is LEAST likely to be a test for asphalt is   11.____

A. specific gravity   B. flashpoint
C. viscosity   D. penetration

12. According to the AASHO, for bituminous pavements PSI is an abbreviation for _____   12.____
Index.

A. Present Serviceability   B. Pavement Smoothness
C. Pavement Serviceability   D. Present Smoothness

13. According to the AASHO, a bituminous pavement that is in extremely poor condition will have a PSI   13.____

A. above 5.5   B. above 3.5
C. below 3.5   D. below 1.5

14. The U.S. Federal Highway Administration defines asphalt maintenance as including work designed primarily for rejuvenation or protection of existing surfaces less than _____ inch minimum thickness.   14.____

A. 1/4   B. 1/2   C. 3/4   D. 1

15. The maintenance phase of a highway management system includes the establishment of a program and schedule of work based largely on budget considerations, the actual operations of crack filling, patching, etc. and   15.____

A. inspection of completed work
B. planning of future operations
C. upgrading existing pavements
D. acquisition and processing of data

16. In a bituminous asphalt pavement, the progressive separation of aggregate particles in a 16.____
pavement from the surface downward or from the edges inward is the definition of

    A. alligatoring   B. raveling
    C. scaling   D. disintegration

17. The bituminous pavement condition for the purpose of overlay design includes ride qual- 17.____
ity, structural capacity, skid resistance, and

    A. durability   B. age of the pavement
    C. CBR value   D. surface distress

18. An asphalt mix is being transferred from an asphalt truck to the hopper of the paving 18.____
machine. Blue smoke rises from the material being emptied into the hopper of the paving
machine.
Your conclusion should be that

    A. this is normal and is to be expected
    B. the mix is overheated
    C. the mix is too cold
    D. the mix is being transferred too rapidly

19. Polished aggregate in an asphalt pavement are aggregate particles that have been 19.____
rounded and polished smooth by traffic. This is a

    A. *good* condition as it allows a smooth ride
    B. *good* condition as it preserves tires
    C. *poor* condition as it promotes skidding
    D. *poor* condition as it tends to break the bond between the asphalt and the aggre-
gate

20. A slippery asphalt surface requires a skid-resistant surfacing material. Of the following, 20.____
the cover that would be most appropriate is a(n)

    A. asphalt tack coat
    B. fog seal
    C. layer of sand rolled into the asphalt surface
    D. asphalt emulsion slurry seal

21. The maximum size of aggregate in a hot mix asphalt concrete surfacing and bases 21.____
allowed by the Federal Highway Administration Grading A is _____ inch(es).

    A. 3/4   B. 1   C. 1 1/4   D. 1 1/2

22. Wet sand weighs 132 pounds per cubic foot and contains 8% noisture. The dry weight of 22.____
a cubic foot of sand is _____ pounds.

    A. 122.2   B. 122.0   C. 121.7   D. 121.4

23. A very light spray application of 551h emulsified asphalt diluted with water is used on 23.____
existing pavement as a seal to riinimize raveling and to enrich the surface of a dried-out
pavement is known as a(n)

    A. prime coat   B. tack coat
    C. fog seal   D. emulsion seal

24. 90 kilometers per hour is equivalent to _____ miles per hour. 24.____

    A. 49   B. 54   C. 59   D. 64

25. In a table of pavement distress manifestations is a column broadly titled *Density of Pave-* 25.____
ment Distress.
This is equivalent to _____ of the defects.

    A. average depth   B. average area
    C. extent of occurrence   D. seriousness

KEY (CORRECT ANSWERS)

1.	A		11.	A
2.	A		12.	A
3.	D		13.	D
4.	C		14.	C
5.	A		15.	D
6.	B		16.	B
7.	B		17.	D
8.	D		18.	B
9.	B		19.	C
10.	C		20.	D

21.	D
22.	A
23.	C
24.	B
25.	C

EXAMINATION SECTION
TEST 1

DIRECTIONS: Each question or incomplete statement is followed by several suggested answers or completions. Select the one that BEST answers the questions or completes the statement. *PRINT THE LETTER OF THE CORRECT ANSWER IN THE SPACE AT THE RIGHT.*

1.   Of the following, the FIRST operation in the demolition of a 4-story building adjacent to the property line is the

    A.   erection of railings around the stairwells
    B.   shoring of adjoining buildings
    C.   erection of a sidewalk shed
    D.   removal of windows

1.____

2.   Projected sash is defined as a(n)

    A.   double hung window
    B.   window that opens inward or outward
    C.   architectural projection from a building exterior
    D.   storm window

2.____

3.   Specifications for a reinforced concrete structure call for a roof fill to be placed on the concrete roof slab. Of the following, the PURPOSE of the fill is to

    A.   reduce sound transmission
    B.   facilitate drainage
    C.   provide a smooth base for insulation
    D.   protect the concrete slab

3.____

4.   The Building Department requires a location survey by a licensed surveyor

    A.   *only* if it is suspected that the building is not in the proper place and may impinge on adjacent property
    B.   *only* of the completed foundation
    C.   *only* of the completed superstructure
    D.   *after* the foundation is completed and a second survey after the building is completed

4.____

5.   After excavating by a contractor for a footing, the sub-grade soil appears to be below the quality shown on the borings.
Of the following types of footings, the one that would be LEAST affected by this condition is a

    A.   spread footing   B.   combined footing
    C.   footing on piles   D.   footing and pier

5.____

6.   Of the following, the information of GREATEST significance to be recorded for each pile during pile driving is the

    A.   steam pressure and the temperature
    B.   condition of the ground at the pile location

6.____

C. number of hammer blows at the last inch
D. total number of hammer blows

7. One method of dewatering an excavation for a foundation is by the use of   7.____

A. inverted siphons   B. well points
C. line holes   D. suction heads

8. An excavation for a concrete footing to support a structural steel column was dug 4" too   8.____
deep.
Of the following, the BEST construction practice would be to

A. backfill the 4" with stone
B. backfill the 4" with sand
C. lower the entire footing 4"
D. make the footing 4" thicker

9. Spudding, in a pile driving operation, is used PRIMARILY to   9.____

A. remove a broken pile
B. pass an obstruction
C. compact the soil in the area
D. splice piles

10. Where walers and form ties are used in wood formwork for tall vertical concrete walls, the   10.____
walers are

A. more closely spaced at the top of the wall than at the bottom
B. evenly spaced at the top to the bottom of the wall
C. more closely spaced at the bottom of the wall than at the top
D. more closely spaced at the middle of the wall than at either the top or the bottom

11. A non-bearing wall unit between columns enclosing a structure is known as a _____   11.____
wall.

A. panel   B. curtain
C. apron   D. spandrel

12. In a multi-story building, standpipes are installed FIRST by the plumber for   12.____

A. water supply   B. sanitary facilities
C. fire protection   D. steam supply

13. It is necessary to burn reinforcing steel while they are in the wood forms in order to   13.____
change their lengths.
The STANDARD safety precaution to observe during this process is to

A. fireproof the wood forms
B. use a low heat flame
C. have a man stand by with a fire extinguisher
D. soak a 20-foot radius around the area with water

14. Specifications for a building require that the first floor beams must be in place before   14.____
backfilling against the foundation walls.
Of the following, the BEST reason for this requirement is that

    A.   the utilities up to the first floor level should be in place before backfilling
    B.   without the first floor beams in place, the wall may become overstressed
    C.   it facilitates the inspection of the first floor construction
    D.   it facilitates the inspection of the backfilling operation

15. The utility line that USUALLY enters the building at the *lowest* elevation is the   15.____

    A.   electric cable   B.   gas lines
    C.   water lines   D.   plumbing drain

16. Specifications for a building require that machine excavation for foundation footings be   16.____
within a foot of final subgrade and the remaining excavation be done by hand. Of the following, the BEST reasons for this requirement is to

    A.   prevent cave-ins around the excavation
    B.   save the amount of fill needed
    C.   prevent disturbing the surrounding excavation
    D.   prevent excavation below the subgrade

17. Of the following outside lines entering a building, the one for which grades must be   17.____
MOST carefully controlled is the

    A.   sewer line   B.   water line
    C.   gas line   D.   electric cable

18. On a plan, the grades for a building are as follows: 18.____
    Datum $\pm$ 0 (Elev. 24.08')
    First floor El + 1' - 0" (Elev. 25.08').
The elevation of a ledge 6'3" below the finished first floor level with respect to datum is

    A.   El. - 6.25   B.   El. - 5.25
    C.   El. + 18.83   D.   El. + 17.83

19. Specifications for a building call for *defective material to be removed from the job site*   19.____
immediately. The MAIN reason for this is to

    A.   prevent accidents
    B.   prevent accidental use of the defective material in the construction
    C.   insure that the contractor does not make the same mistake again
    D.   minimize claims against the department

20. *Drywall* is installed by   20.____

    A.   carpenters   B.   lathers
    C.   plasterers   D.   masons

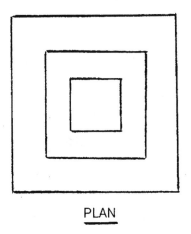

PLAN

21. The Plan of a footing and concrete column is shown above. An elevation of the footing would be shown as: 21.____

A.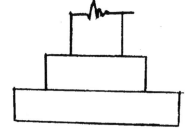

B.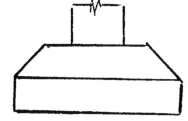

C.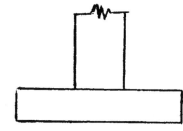

D.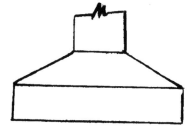

22. Of the following, the BEST sequence to follow in pouring the interior footing, concrete column and basement floor as shown below is pour the footing,   22.____

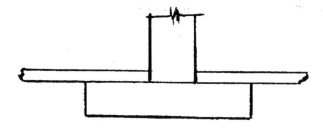

    A. and floor in one pour. Pour the column
    B. and column in one pour. Pour the floor
    C. pour the floor above the footing, pour the column above the floor
    D. box out for the floor, pour the column. Pour the floor

23. The PURPOSE of curing concrete is so that the 23.____

    A. forms for the concrete can be stripped quickly
    B. water content will not evaporate too quickly
    C. concrete will harden faster
    D. reinforcing rods will not rust

24. Air-entraining cement may be required so that the resulting concrete will resist 24.____

    A. freezing and thawing   B. hot weather
    C. dampness   D. heavy loads

25. Concrete test cylinders are required to 25.____

    A. provide an indication of the strength of the concrete poured in a specific location
    B. provide a basis of payment
    C. check on the inspector
    D. check the source of material

26. Concrete test cylinders are stored and cured on the job 26.____

    A. so that the contractor can then control the curing
    B. so that the inspector can then control the curing
    C. because the laboratory has no facilities for curing concrete cylinders
    D. because conditions of curing on the job are the same as at the location poured

27. The *water-cement ratio* refers to the quantity of water in a concrete mix as 27.____

    A. cubic feet of water per cubic foot of cement
    B. gallons of water per pound of cement
    C. gallons of water per sack of cement
    D. bags of cement per gallon of water

28. *Slump* of concrete refers to the 28.____

    A. shrinkage of concrete while setting
    B. drop in height relative to a standard testing cone
    C. amount of water introduced into the concrete
    D. cracking or crazing of the surface of concrete

29. Concrete mixes made with lightweight aggregate USUALLY require the addition of an air-entraining agent in order to 29.____

    A. increase the strength of the concrete
    B. reduce the weight of the concrete
    C. obtain the necessary plasticity without added water
    D. save aggregate material

30. Concrete in some instances requires integral waterproofing.
This can BEST be achieved by 30.____

    A. addition of more cement in the mix
    B. longer vibration
    C. addition of a waterproofing agent to the mix
    D. longer curing period

31. In placing concrete where the vertical drop is greater than 5 feet, the use of an elephant   31._____
trunk is necessary.
The BEST reason for using an elephant trunk is to

    A. prevent segregation of the aggregate
    B. prevent waste of material
    C. safeguard health and property
    D. save time and labor

32. According to the Building Code, the maximum size of coarse aggregate for reinforced   32._____
concrete shall be one-fifth of the narrowest dimension between forms or three-quarters
of the clear spacing between reinforcing bars. Of the following, the MAXIMUM sized
aggregate permitted for a 12" wall with #6 bars spaced at 3" center to center is

    A. 1 3/4"   B. 1 1/2"   C. 1 1/4"   D. 1"

33. Of the following, the one that is NOT a name for a lightweight aggregate is   33._____

    A. Solite   B. Vitralite
    C. Lelite   D. Nitralite

34. High early strength cement is designated as   34._____

    A. Type I   B. Type II   C. Type III   D. Type IV

35. The average weight of stone concrete is, MOST NEARLY, _____ lb./cu. ft.   35._____

    A. 125   B. 150
    C. 175   D. 200

KEY (CORRECT ANSWERS)

1.	C	16.	D
2.	B	17.	A
3.	B	18.	B
4.	D	19.	B
5.	C	20.	A
6.	C	21.	A
7.	B	22.	D
8.	D	23.	B
9.	B	24.	A
10.	C	25.	A
11.	B	26.	D
12.	C	27.	C
13.	C	28.	B
14.	B	29.	C
15.	D	30.	C

31.	A
32.	B
33.	B
34.	C
35.	B

TEST 2

DIRECTIONS: Each question or incomplete statement is followed by several suggested answers or completions. Select the one that BEST answers the question or completes the statement. *PRINT THE LETTER OF THE CORRECT ANSWER IN THE SPACE AT THE RIGHT.*

1. The Building Code requires that concrete shall be kept in a moist condition, after placing, for at least the FIRST _____ days.

    A. 3   B. 7   C. 14   D. 28

1.____

2. In concrete work, a dummy joint is SIMILAR in purpose to a(n) _____ joint.

    A. expansion   B. construction
    C. contraction   D. shear

2.____

3. Specifications for concrete usually contain a statement disallowing the *retampering* of concrete. *Retampering* means

    A. adding more water to the drum after ingredients are mixed
    B. vibrating of concrete in the forms
    C. mixing of the remaining concrete after some concrete is taken from the truck
    D. mixing of concrete in the truck after it has partially set and adding water

3.____

4. Chamfers are placed on a concrete beam PRIMARILY to

    A. save weight   B. eliminate honeycomb
    C. eliminate sharp corners   D. save construction costs

4.____

5. Of the following, the BEST reason for using vibrators in concrete construction is to

    A. increase the workability of the concrete
    B. consolidate the concrete
    C. slow up the setting
    D. speed up the setting

5.____

6. The concrete test that will BEST determine the consistency of a concrete mix is the

    A. sieve analysis   B. water-cement ratio test
    C. calorimetric test   D. slump test

6.____

7. Specifications for the concrete floor treatment of a building require *dustproofing*. This process consists of

    A. scraping the floor surface to remove loose concrete material that will dust
    B. mopping the floor with a chemical solution that will harden the concrete surface
    C. adding a chemical compound to the concrete mix that will harden the surface of the concrete
    D. grinding the concrete floor with a terrazzo machine that will case harden the surface of the concrete

7.____

8. In checking the placement of reinforcing steel, it is discovered that reinforcing steel called for on the design drawings is not shown on the reinforcing steel shop drawings. Of the following, the BEST procedure to follow is to

8.____

    A.   check the design drawings for the errors
    B.   check the shop drawings for the errors
    C.   subtract the missing steel in the field
    D.   stop all work

9.   While a large spread footing of about 50 cubic yards Is being poured, the supply plant   9.____
breaks down. Concrete is available from another supplier.
The use of the other supplier should

    A.   not be approved because the supplier may not be approved
    B.   be approved since additional test cylinders can be taken
    C.   not be approved since construction joints can be installed where the pour has
        ended
    D.   be approved as the concrete in footings is relatively unimportant

10.   Of the following species of lumber, the one MOST likely to be used for concrete formwork   10.____
is

    A.   oak   B.   pine   C.   maple   D.   birch

11.   A contractor proposes to install the roofing two days after the concrete roof slab is   11.____
poured.
This proposal should

    A.   *be recommended* as it will speed the construction
    B.   *be recommended* as it will cure the concrete better
    C.   *not be recommended* as excess water may bulge the roofing
    D.   *not be recommended* in cold weather but would be recommended in warm weather

12.   For the construction of concrete floors resting on earth, the item that should be MOST   12.____
carefully checked is that

    A.   the earth is dry before pouring
    B.   the earth is wet before pouring
    C.   all backfill is properly compacted
    D.   all backfill is porous soil

13.   Cracks in concrete are not necessarily caused by settlement of a structure.   13.____
Sometimes they are caused by

    A.   shrinkage   B.   plastic flow
    C.   hydration   D.   curing

14.   Specifications for a building state that reinforcing bars must lap 40 diameters in the con-   14.____
crete.
The length of lap for a number 6 bar should be, MOST NEARLY, _____ inches.

    A.   12   B.   20   C.   30   D.   40

15.   Cement stored on the job site that has become caked and lumpy may   15.____

    A.   be used only for foundations
    B.   be used only for slabs on ground
    C.   be used anywhere if the lumps are broken up
    D.   not be used

16. Of the following statements relating to the plies in plywood, the one that is CORRECT is: 16.____

    A. The primary difference between exterior and interior plywood is the quality of the exterior plies.
    B. Exterior plywood has more plies than interior plywood.
    C. Exterior plywood has no surface defects on the outer plies while interior plywood permits surface defects on the outer plies.
    D. Plywood has an odd number of plies.

17. Of the following, the one that is NOT a principal classification of lumber according to the American Lumber Standards is   17.____

    A. building   B. structural
    C. yard   D. shop

18. Of the following types of lumber, the one that is classified as a hardwood is   18.____

    A. cedar   B. fir   C. pine   D. maple

19. When building the formwork for a 12" doubly reinforced concrete wall, the USUAL order of conctruction is to place the   19.____

    A. formwork for both faces of the wall; then place the steel
    B. formwork for one face of the wall, place all reinforcing steel, then place the form-work for the other face of the wall
    C. reinforcing steel, then place the formwork for both faces of the wall
    D. formwork for one face of the wall, place the reinforcing steel for one face, place the form-work for the other face of the wall, then place the reinforcing steel for the second face

20. To obtain information concerning the product of a particular major manufacturer of flooring, the BEST of the following sources of information is the   20.____

    A. Architectural Standards   B. ASTM
    C. Sweet's Catalogue   D. Flooring Institute

21. Of the following, loose lintels would MOST likely be found in the specifications under the item entitled   21.____

    A. Ornamental Iron   B. Miscellaneous Iron
    C. Structural Steel   D. Hollow Metal Work

22. Galvanized metal lath is metal lath coated with   22.____

    A. tin   B. copper   C. zinc   D. nickel

23. In the welding symbol the 2 represents the   23.____
    A. spacing between welds in inches
    B. length of the weld in inches
    C. number of sides to be welded
    D. thickness of the throat of the weld in inches

24. The specification for a building states that rib lath should be 3.4 pounds. This MEANS 3.4 pounds per   24._____

    A. square foot
    B. linear foot of a 3 foot roll
    C. square yard
    D. 10 square feet

25. Terrazzo floors are laid with brass dividing strips PRIMARILY for the purpose of   25._____

    A. preventing slipping
    B. appearance
    C. preventing irregular cracking
    D. easy screeding

26. The PURPOSE of a chase is to   26._____

    A. support stair stringers
    B. accomodate pipes in a wall
    C. accomodate flashing in a parapet
    D. provide venting

27. In masonry work, a bull nose brick would be located at   27._____

    A. an inside corner   B. an outside corner
    C. the key of an arch   D. the roof of a boiler setting

28. The addition of lime to cement mortar improves the workability of mortar and   28._____

    A. increases the strength
    B. decreases the shrinkage
    C. decreases the weight
    D. increases the watertightness

29. Brickwork must be cleaned after completion of setting by   29._____

    A. scrubbing with soap solution and water
    B. wire brushing
    C. washing with muriatic solution
    D. sand blasting

30. In a multi-story building, weep holes in cavity wall brick construction are USUALLY placed in the brickwork   30._____

    A. above all masonry openings
    B. at foundation level only
    C. at the parapet only
    D. at every floor

31. A brick wall which consists of all stretcher courses is said to be built with a _____ Bond.   31._____

    A. Flemish   B. Running
    C. English   D. Common

32. The whitish deposit frequently seen on brick walls can USUALLY be avoided by   32.____

    A. using brick that contains more soluable salts
    B. keeping the water-mortar ratio high
    C. adding muriatic acid to the mortar
    D. constructing properly filled weathertight joints

33. Specifications for a building require brick to be wet before using.   33.____
    Of the following, the BEST reason for this requirement is that wetting

    A. makes it easier to place brick
    B. cleans the brick
    C. prevents absorption of moisture from the mortar
    D. shows up flaws in the brick that would otherwise be hidden

34. In checking the ingredients that are to go into the concrete for a footing that is being   34.____
    poured, you notice that there is 5% too much cement.
    Of the following, the BEST action to take in this situation is to

    A. do nothing
    B. condemn the footing
    C. increase the amount of sand in the mix
    D. order core borings taken of the finished footing

35. The soil conditions for a new building are MOST frequently checked by   35.____

    A. augering   B. soundings
    C. rodding   D. borings

———————

KEY (CORRECT ANSWERS)

1.	B	16.	D
2.	C	17.	A
3.	D	18.	D
4.	C	19.	B
5.	B	20.	C
6.	D	21.	B
7.	B	22.	C
8.	B	23.	B
9.	B	24.	C
10.	B	25.	C
11.	C	26.	B
12.	C	27.	B
13.	A	28.	B
14.	C	29.	C
15.	D	30.	D

31.	B
32.	D
33.	C
34.	A
35.	D

———

EXAMINATION SECTION
TEST 1

DIRECTIONS: Each question or incomplete statement is followed by several suggested answers or completions. Select the one that BEST answers the question or completes the statement. *PRINT THE LETTER OF THE CORRECT ANSWER IN THE SPACE AT THE RIGHT.*

1. Of the following aggregates, the one LEAST frequently used in the manufacture of light-weight concrete is

    A. cinders   B. slag   C. perlite   D. mica

1.____

2. The purpose of a chase is to

    A. accommodate pipes in a wall
    B. act as a support for a stair stringer
    C. provide clearance between wood frame and a chimney
    D. flash block into a parapet

2.____

3. In masonry work, a bullnose brick would be used at

    A. an inside corner
    B. an outside corner
    C. the key of an arch
    D. the roof of a boiler setting

3.____

4. When asphalt shingles are applied to a sloping roof, a cant strip is frequently used. The purpose of this cant strip is to

    A. prevent leaking at the ridge
    B. hold together opposite sides of a valley
    C. eliminate the possibility of wind lifting the shingles
    D. raise the lower edge of the first course of shingles

4.____

5. Air entrained concrete is used rather than ordinary concrete MAINLY to provide additional resistance to

    A. fire   B. impact
    C. freezing and thawing   D. water penetration

5.____

6. The type of construction MOST commonly used in new wood frame dwellings is the _____ frame.

    A. platform   B. braced   C. balloon   D. butt

6.____

7. Of the following, the one LEAST commonly used for flashing is

    A. copper   B. monel
    C. polyethylene   D. asphalt felt

7.____

8. The end of a wood joist resting directly on a concrete wall has to be brought up to level. The BEST material to use as a shim for this purpose is

    A. slate   B. wood shingles
    C. dressed wood   D. grout

8.____

9. In foundation work, an example of a rock that would be considered a SOFT rock is   9.____

    A. gneiss   B. granite   C. shale   D. limestone

10. Segregation in concrete will result from improper   10.____

    A. curing   B. placing   C. formwork   D. finishing

11. One method of dewatering an excavation for a foundation is the use of   11.____

    A. inverted siphons   B. line holes
    C. well points   D. suction heads

12. An excavation for a concrete footing to support a steel column was accidentally dug 4"   12.____
    too deep.
    Of the following, the BEST practice would be to

    A. make the footing 4" thicker
    B. backfill the 4" with stone
    C. backfill the 4" with clean sand and puddle the fill carefully
    D. lower the footing 4"

13. The MOST common finish for a concrete walk is a _____ finish.   13.____

    A. steel trowel   B. screeded
    C. sealed   D. wood float

14. In setting diagonal cross bridging on wood joists, the BEST method is to   14.____

    A. nail at top and bottom before subflooring is in place
    B. nail at bottom, place subflooring, then nail at top
    C. nail at top, place subflooring, then nail at bottom
    D. place subflooring, then nail at top and bottom

15. In a fireproof building, purlins used to support a suspended ceiling are USUALLY   15.____

    A. T   B. channel   C. I   D. lattice

16. *Standing seams* are MOST frequently found in _____ roofs.   16.____

    A. built up   B. poured gypsum
    C. copper   D. concrete plank

17. Long span steel floor joists differ from ordinary light steel beams used as joists in that the   17.____
    long span joists

    A. come with welded plank clips on the top flange
    B. do not require fireproofing
    C. have lower flanges with adaptors for suspended ceilings
    D. have open diagonal lacing rather than solid webs

18. In fireproofing steel girders (4 hour fire rating), the minimum thickness of concrete (ordi-   18.____
    nary concrete made with trap rock) required to protect the girder is

    A. 1"   B. 2"   C. 3"   D. 4"

19. The base composition of plaster boards is
19.____

    A. cement
    B. vermiculite
    C. gypsum
    D. perlite

20. In the ordinary cantilever type retaining wall, the main steel reinforcing in the upright part will be _____ and nearest the side of the wall _____ the earth.
20.____

    A. vertical; next to
    B. horizontal; next to
    C. vertical; away from
    D. horizontal; away from

21. A major disadvantage in the use of lime mortar for brickwork is that the lime
21.____

    A. sets too slowly
    B. is too difficult to apply
    C. discolors the brick too much
    D. reduces the fire resistance of the masonry

22. Mortar joints in old brick walls are BEST repaired by
22.____

    A. setting
    B. framing
    C. taping
    D. pointing

23. Of the following, the MAIN advantage of a 10" brick cavity wall over an 8" solid brick wall is that the cavity wall
23.____

    A. is stronger
    B. resists rain penetration better
    C. is not affected by freezing and thawing
    D. can be used with more varieties of bond

24. In large metropolitan cities, masonry structural units are considered *solid* structural units when they are (select SMALLEST acceptable value) _____ *solid*.
24.____

    A. 70%
    B. 75%
    C. 80%
    D. 85%

25. The PRIMARY function of a vapor barrier is to
25.____

    A. stop water from entering the space between a parapet wall and a roof surface
    B. prevent a driving rain from penetrating a roof surface
    C. seal openings around a hot water pipe in a wall
    D. block moisture in warm air from entering unheated ceiling and wall spaces

KEY (CORRECT ANSWERS)

1.	D		11.	C
2.	A		12.	A
3.	B		13.	D
4.	D		14.	C
5.	C		15.	B
6.	A		16.	C
7.	B		17.	D
8.	A		18.	B
9.	C		19.	C
10.	B		20.	A

21.	A
22.	D
23.	B
24.	B
25.	D

TEST 2

DIRECTIONS: Each question or incomplete statement is followed by several suggested answers or completions. Select the one that BEST answers the question or completes the statement. *PRINT THE LETTER OF THE CORRECT ANSWER IN THE SPACE AT THE RIGHT.*

1. On a plan, the symbol ⊥⊥⊥ represents

1._____

    A. brick
    B. cinder concrete block
    C. hollow clay tile
    D. gypsum block

2. Where a continuous concrete floor slab is supported on concrete beams and girders, poured integrally, the BEST place to make a construction joint is at a point

2._____

    A. midway between the beams
    B. directly over the center of a beam
    C. a distance from the face of the beam equal to the depth of the beam
    D. one-third of the distance from the face of the beam to the center of the beam

3. If legal curb grade is at elevation 134.27, and the first floor level is 4'2 1/4" above legal curb grade, then the elevation of the first floor is MOST NEARLY

3._____

    A. 138.40   B. 138.42   C. 138.44   D. 138.46

4. Of the following practices, the one that is MOST likely to result in segregation in concrete is

4._____

    A. inadequate floating
    B. vibrating mixes that can be readily consolidated by hand
    C. placing the chutes in such a way that the discharge end is always at the end of the fresh concrete surface
    D. placing the concrete in thin layers over the entire area to be concreted

5. Stone sills frequently have a groove cut into the underside.
This is done MAINLY to

5._____

    A. assist in anchoring the sill with clips
    B. allow flashing to be inserted
    C. give the mortar a *key* or grip
    D. prevent rain dripping onto the wall

6. A permit to store paint in quantities greater than 20 gallons must be obtained from the

6._____

    A. Police Department
    B. Department of Air Resources
    C. Fire Department
    D. Building Department

7. The specifications state that glass shall have a thickness of 1/8" 1/32".
Of the following thicknesses of glass, the one that does NOT meet the above specification is

7._____

    A. .090"   B. .110"   C. .130"   D. .150"

8. Of the following, the one that designates a quality of clear glass is   8.____

   A. Class II   B. B
   C. select grade   D. transparent

9. A section of the specifications calls for concrete fill. This concrete is MOST likely to be   9.____
   _____ concrete.

   A. reinforced   B. high early strength
   C. cinder   D. sulfate resisting

10. When concrete is to have a rubbed finish,   10.____

   A. the concrete must be thoroughly dry before the rubbing operation commences
   B. mortar is usually used in the rubbing operation
   C. grout is usually used in the rubbing operation
   D. the surfaces should be kept thoroughly wet during rubbing operations

11. The specification for Average *A* concrete is as follows: 11.____

   A. 1:1:3   B. 1:2:3 1/2   C. 1:2:4   D. 1:1 1/2:3

12. The specification states: *The value of each change order shall be computed separately*   12.____
    by cost of labor and materials, plus equipment allowance, plus overhead and profit.

    The MOST probable value of overhead and profit is _____ of the cost of labor and
    materials plus equipment allowance.

   A. 5%   B. 15%   C. 34%   D. 55%

13. In the specifications is an item, *Equipment Allowance: Shall include rental of necessary*   13.____
    equipment plus 9% of this rental.
    According to the above specification, if a piece of equipment rents for $35 per day,
    Equipment Allowance for this equipment rented for 11 days is MOST NEARLY

   A. $484.00   B. $378.42   C. $385.00   D. $419.65

14. Plank clips that are .062 inches thick are MOST NEARLY _____ thick.   14.____

   A. 1/32"   B. 2/32"   C. 3/32"   D. 4/32"

15. Of the following types of structured steel shapes, the one of the following that is UNLIKE   15.____
    the others in general is

   A. W   B. H   C. I   D. T

16. Terra cotta is composed primarily of   16.____

   A. limestone   B. portland cement
   C. gypsum   D. clay

17. In the specification for brickwork is a paragraph entitled *bond.*   17.____
    With reference to brickwork, bond refers to

   A. the pattern of the brickwork
   B. the guarantee of the life of the brick

C. the mortar joining the brick
D. water tightness of the brick wall

18. The specifications for the laying of block state that the joint shall be slightly concave. 18.____
This would appear MOST likely as in

A.   B.   C.   D.

19. The maximum size of a sand particle beyond which it is NOT considered sand is _____ 19.____
inch.

   A. 1/16   B. 1/8   C. 3/16   D. 1/4

20. The specifications state that concrete shall have an ultimate compressive strength of 20.____
4000 psi. This means the compressive strength at the end of _____ days.

   A. 7   B. 14   C. 21   D. 28

21. The primary purpose of curing a freshly poured concrete slab is to _____ the concrete. 21.____

   A. prevent loss of water from
   B. minimize segregation in
   C. minimize honeycombing in
   D. prevent efflorescense in

22. Silicone water repellent would MOST likely be used on 22.____

   A. the inside of a foundation wall
   B. the outside of a foundation wall
   C. an exposed brick wall
   D. the roof of a building

23. *Parging* of a brick wall is also known as 23.____

   A. buttering   B. backplastering
   C. slushing   D. scratching

24. The specifications require 2.2 lbs. metal lath. The 2.2 lbs. represents the weight per 24.____

   A. foot   B. yard
   C. square foot   D. square yard

25. Cleaning of glazed surfaces of a completed structural facing tile surface is BEST done by 25.____

   A. sandblasting
   B. washing with soap powder in boiling water
   C. wire brushing
   D. scrubbing with a medium solution of muriatic acid

KEY (CORRECT ANSWERS)

1.	B		11.	C
2.	A		12.	B
3.	D		13.	D
4.	B		14.	B
5.	D		15.	D
6.	C		16.	D
7.	A		17.	A
8.	B		18.	A
9.	C		19.	D
10.	D		20.	D

21. A
22. C
23. B
24. D
25. B

———

TEST 3

DIRECTIONS: Each question or incomplete statement is followed by several suggested answers or completions. Select the one that BEST answers the question or completes the statement. *PRINT THE LETTER OF THE CORRECT ANSWER IN THE SPACE AT THE RIGHT.*

1. A metal support for plaster is 1 1/4" x 1/2" x 1/8". The 1/2" refers to

   A. A
   B. B
   C. C
   D. D

   1._____

2. The specification requires stove bolts.
   The head of a stove bolt would MOST LIKELY appear as in

   A.   B.   C.   D.

   2._____

3. In a hung plaster ceiling, the metal lath is tied to the

   A. runner   B. hanger
   C. tee insert   D. cross furring

   3._____

4. Plastering has just been completed in a room.
   The proper way to ventilate the room to dry out the plaster when the outside weather conditions are moderate is to

   A. keep the window shut
   B. open the bottom window all the way
   C. open the top and bottom window 2 inches
   D. open the top window all the way

   4._____

5. The specification for a wood door states: *Stiles and rails of doors M & T together and assembled with hardwood wedges.*
   M & T stands for

   A. mitred and tongued   B. matches and tacked
   C. milled and tacked   D. mortise and tenon

   5._____

6. The weight of a gallon of ordinary paint, in pounds, is MOST NEARLY

   A. 5   B. 13   C. 21   D. 29

   6._____

7. A section in the specification is entitled *Resilient Flooring.*
   Of the following types of flooring, the one that is NOT considered resilient flooring is

   A. linoleum   B. asphalt tile
   C. vinyl asbestos tile   D. quarry tile

   7._____

8. The specifications state: *All exposed surfaces shall be free from knot spots, spalls, ohips, and mineral stains.* The material referred to is MOST likely

   A. brick   B. wood   C. marble   D. quarry tile

   8._____

9. A protective transparent coating is to be placed on the aluminum surface of an aluminum window.   9.____
The coating would MOST likely be a transparent coating of

    A. gum arable   B. shellac
    C. stain   D. lacquer

10. The vertical side of a window frame is known as the   10.____

    A. sill   B. muntin   C. rail   D. jamb

11. The specifications state: *Sill and head shall be No. 12 B & S gauge minimum.*   11.____
B & S is an abbreviation of

    A. Black & Stone   B. Birmingham & Stone
    C. Black & Sloane   D. Brown & Sharpe

12. In three coat plaster, the finish coat follows the brown coat.   12.____
The minimum number of days that must elapse after the brown coat is completed before the finish coat may be applied is MOST NEARLY

    A. 1   B. 3   C. 17   D. 32

13. Of the following, the method of construction that is encountering difficulty with governmental agencies because of environmental pollution is   13.____

    A. guniting
    B. spray painting
    C. sprayed on insulation
    D. air entraining of concrete

14. The specifications on piping require the use of graphite on cleanout plugs.   14.____
Of the following, the BEST reason for the use of graphite is to

    A. facilitate installing the plug
    B. facilitate removing the plug
    C. make the plug watertight
    D. give the plug a dark color for identification purposes

15. The specifications state that the concrete shall have a certain minimum *cement factor.*   15.____
Cement factor is the

    A. number of bags of cement per cubic yard of concrete
    B. gallons of water per bag of cement
    C. number of bags of cement per gallon of water
    D. slump of the concrete

16. The specifications state that the ends of a wood beam shall be firecut.   16.____
The end of the beam would appear in place as shown in

    A.   B.   C.   D.

17. One of the unit price items in the contract for extra or omitted work in a building is rein-   17.____
forcing steel in place.
This price is MOST likely _____ /pound.

    A. 12¢   B. 22¢   C. 32¢   D. 42¢

18. The specifications require that porous fill be placed under a concrete slab.   18.____
The material LEAST likely to be permitted as porous fill is

    A. crushed stone   B. sand
    C. gravel   D. loam

19. Of the following, the organization NOT concerned with standards for construction mate-   19.____
rial is

    A. A.I.S.C.   B. A.C.I.   C. A.S.T.M.   D. A.I.E.M.

20. The specification on grouting states: *The contractor shall furnish all material and labor for*   20.____
properly bedding on Portland cement grout, the equipment or its supporting base.
Grout of this type would usually consist of

    A. Portland cement only
    B. 1 part Portland cement and 1 part sand
    C. 1 part Portland cement and 4 parts sand
    D. 1 part Portland cement and 8 parts sand

21. Referring to the above question, the thickness of grout for the bases of machinery and   21.____
equipment normally found in buildings would be, in inches, MOST NEARLY _____
inch(es).

    A. 1/4   B. 1/2   C. 1   D. 3

22. One of the duties of a superintendent is to keep a record of all delays caused by strikes,   22.____
walkouts, rain, or other causes beyond the contractor's control.
Of the following, the BEST reason for keeping this record is to

    A. penalize the contractor for delays
    B. enable the city to plan future jobs more accurately
    C. allow the contractor additional time to complete the contract when necessary
    D. require the contractor to put on additional forces to meet the contract deadline

23. In setting, the reinforcing steel for a concrete slab 3/8" temperature reinforcing rod inter-   23.____
fered with a one inch vertical sleeve for a cold water line. The contractor moved the temperature bar 1/2 inch at the sleeve to avoid the interference.
This action on the part of the contractor was

    A. *improper,* since the bar should have been cut at the point of interference
    B. *improper,* since the layout of all the 3/8 inch bars was incorrect according to the
plans
    C. *proper,* because very minor changes in location of temperature reinforcing steel is
permissible
    D. *proper,* because cutting steel and placing additional reinforcing steel around the
opening would weaken the slab

24. Of the following permits for a new school building, the one NOT issued by the department   24.____
of buildings is the pernit to

    A. build
    B. install elevators
    C. erect sidewalk shed when necessary
    D. store material on sidewalk

25. A reinforced concrete canopy is to be   25.____
constructed. The reinforcing steel would
MOST likely appear as in

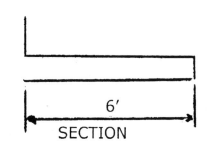

SECTION

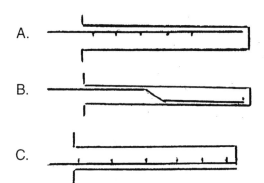

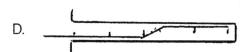

KEY (CORRECT ANSWERS)

1.	B	11.	D
2.	B	12.	B
3.	D	13.	C
4.	C	14.	B
5.	D	15.	A
6.	B	16.	C
7.	D	17.	B
8.	C	18.	D
9.	D	19.	D
10.	D	20.	B

21.	C
22.	C
23.	C
24.	D
25.	A

EXAMINATION SECTION
TEST 1

DIRECTIONS: Each question or incomplete statement is followed by several suggested answers or completions. Select the one that BEST answers the question or completes the statement. *PRINT THE LETTER OF THE CORRECT ANSWER IN THE SPACE AT THE RIGHT.*

1. Construction joints in the concrete columns of a multistory building of flat slab concrete design are located

    A. in the middle of the column
    B. 1 foot above the floor level
    C. at the underside of the floor slab
    D. 1 foot below the floor level

1.____

2. When using wellpoints to dewater an excavation, the well-points are USUALLY set in place by _____ the wellpoints.

    A. hammering   B. jetting
    C. drilling a hole for   D. jacking

2.____

3. In fireproofing steel girders for a four-hour fire rating, the MINIMUM thickness of concrete required to protect the girder is

    A. 1"   B. 2"   C. 3"   D. 4"

3.____

4. When finishing a concrete surface such as a ceiling or column where the concrete is not to be rubbed, voids, honeycombs, and imperfections should NORMALLY be filled with

    A. concrete with a maximum aggregate size of 1/2 inch
    B. concrete fill with a maximum aggregate size of 1/4 inch
    C. gunite
    D. neat cement mortar

4.____

5. The formwork for exposed exterior concrete should be removed

    A. as soon as possible after pouring
    B. when the concrete has reached 3/4 of its design strength
    C. 7 days after pouring
    D. 28 days after pouring

5.____

6. Parging is a term MOST closely associated with

    A. steel work   B. excavation
    C. roofing   D. brickwork

6.____

7. A length of pipe is slipped over a wrench to help remove a stuck coupling. This procedure

    A. should never be used
    B. is acceptable since it gives more leverage
    C. is acceptable if the pipe is tight fitting on the wrench
    D. may be used when a larger wrench is unavailable

7.____

8. The exposed face of precast concrete units should be cleaned with a   8.____

    A. dilute solution of muriatic acid
    B. solution of soap and water
    C. boric acid solution made up of water and sodium borate
    D. dilute solution of nitric acid

9. A sheet of polyethylene plastic is placed over the earth subgrade of a concrete floor   9.____
before the concrete floor is poured.
The MAIN purpose of this plastic covering is to

    A. minimize settlement of the concrete floor
    B. act as a vapor barrier
    C. prevent loss of water from the wet concrete
    D. prevent bleeding of the wet concrete

10. When structural facing tile must be cut in the field, the BEST tool to use is a   10.____

    A. power-driven hacksaw
    B. motor-driven jigsaw
    C. motor-driven steel circular saw
    D. motor-driven carborundum saw

11. Of the following, the type of equipment MOST suitable for making a large, deep excava-   11.____
tion in soft earth where truck ramps cannot be used is a

    A. bulldozer
    B. clamshell bucket on a crane
    C. power shovel
    D. backhoe

12. In a pile-driving operation, spudding is used PRIMARILY to   12.____

    A. remove a broken pile
    B. increase the length of a pile
    C. compact the soil in the area
    D. get past a subsurface obstruction

13. Of the following, the MOST important information to be recorded for each pile during pile   13.____
driving is the

    A. number of hammer blows at the final inch
    B. total number of hammer blows
    C. steam pressure and temperature
    D. condition of the ground at the pile location

14. In the city, *drywall* is installed by   14.____

    A. plasterers   B. carpenters
    C. bricklayers   D. cement masons

15. After pouring concrete in a building in freezing weather, the concrete is USUALLY kept   15.____
from freezing by

    A. heating with live steam
    B. using hot water in the mix
    C. using salamanders and tarpaulins
    D. adding calcium chloride to mix

16. Where wood walers and form ties are used in formwork for a tall vertical concrete wall,   16.____
the walers should be

    A. evenly spaced from the top to the bottom of the wall
    B. more closely spaced at the top of the wall than at the bottom
    C. more closely spaced at the bottom of the wall than at the top
    D. more closely spaced at the middle of the wall than at the top and bottom

17. In a school building, precast concrete plank would MOST likely be used in   17.____

    A. a roof
    B. demountable partitions
    C. the foundation footings
    D. the foundation walls

18. Good construction practice requires that ordinary concrete be kept moist after placing for   18.____
a minimum of _____
day(s).

    A. 1
    B. 2
    C. 7
    D. 28

19. *Retempering* of concrete is prohibited during a concrete pour.   19.____
Retempering means

    A. adding extra cement to the mix before it leaves the mixer
    B. adding extra aggregate to the mix before it leaves the mixer
    C. increasing mixing time
    D. mixing concrete in the mixer after it has partially set

20. Of the following, the MOST important item to consider when a concrete slab is to be sup-   20.____
ported by the earth is whether the earth is

    A. properly compacted
    B. sufficiently porous
    C. wet before pouring the concrete
    D. thoroughly dry before pouring the concrete

21. When placing concrete, a vibrator should be used to   21.____

    A. prevent segregation in the concrete
    B. consolidate the concrete
    C. increase the air content in the concrete
    D. help move the concrete in the forms

22. Of the following, the problem that occurs MOST frequently during the construction of a   22.____
school building is

    A. cracking of the concrete
    B. cracking of the brickwork

C. interference between ductwork and piping
D. settlement of the foundation

23. Upon excavation to subgrade for a pile-supported footing, inspection shows that the soil   23.____
is inferior to that anticipated.
Of the following, the PROPER action for the superintendent representing the contracting agency to take is to

A. stop the job at once
B. notify the engineer to redesign the foundation
C. continue work
D. excavate to a deeper level

24. Of the following, the DOMINANT trade employed in driving precast concrete piles would   24.____
be

A. oilers   B. dockbuilders
C. carpenters   D. concrete workers

25. Reinforcing steel for a footing resting on earth can BEST be held at the specified dis-   25.____
tance above the earth by means of

A. concrete blocks   B. chairs
C. bolsters   D. hangers

KEY (CORRECT ANSWERS)

1.	C	11.	B
2.	B	12.	D
3.	B	13.	A
4.	D	14.	B
5.	A	15.	C
6.	D	16.	C
7.	A	17.	A
8.	B	18.	C
9.	B	19.	D
10.	D	20.	A

21.	B
22.	C
23.	C
24.	B
25.	A

TEST 2

DIRECTIONS: Each question or incomplete statement is followed by several suggested answers or completions. Select the one that BEST answers the question or completes the statement. *PRINT THE LETTER OF THE CORRECT ANSWER IN THE SPACE AT THE RIGHT.*

1. Recently there has been a great deal of discussion of the hazards caused by which of the following chemicals?   1._____

   A. Vinyl chloride
   B. Methyl methacrylate
   C. Sodium pentathol
   D. Formic acid

2. OSHA is the abbreviation for   2._____

   A. Office of Safety Health Administration
   B. Office of State Health Administration
   C. Occupational Standard for Health Administration
   D. Occupational Safety and Health Act

3. Buildings adjacent to a new construction site are pile supported.
   Of the following, the BEST practice to follow in order to defend the city against possible damage claims from owners of the buildings adjacent to the construction site is to   3._____

   A. make a survey of the condition of the adjacent buildings prior to construction at the site
   B. underpin the adjacent buildings in order to be certain that the buildings won't settle
   C. shore the adjacent buildings before excavation begins
   D. insure the adjacent buildings against damage by the contractor

4. One of the requirements of OSHA for building construction jobs is that   4._____

   A. goggles must always be worn
   B. no loose clothing is permitted
   C. hard hats must always be worn
   D. each employee must pass a first aid course

5. Of the following, the INITIAL operation in the demolition of an existing building four stories high whose front face is adjacent to the property line is the   5._____

   A. removal of all windows
   B. shoring of adjoining buildings
   C. boarding up of all openings
   D. erection of a sidewalk shed

6. A plan for the hiring of minority workers on construction projects in the New York area is known as the   6._____

   A. New York Plan
   B. Apprenticeship Program
   C. Board of Urban Affairs Plan
   D. Mayor's Executive Order No. 71

43

7. If there is a discrepancy between the plans and specifications for a construction job, the superintendent representing the contracting agency SHOULD

    A. always follow the plans
    B. always follow the specifications
    C. follow the plans for dimensions only
    D. ask his superior for an interpretation

7.____

8. The specification for a school building contract states under information to bidders: No verbal answer will be given to any inquiries in regard to the meaning of the drawings and specifications, nor will any verbal instructions be given previous to the award of the contract. No verbal statement regarding the contract by any person previous to the award of the contract will be authoritative. Any explanation desired by bidders must be requested in writing. If reply is made, it will be communicated to all contractors who have indicated their intention to bid on the work.
Of the following, the MAIN purpose of the above statement is to

    A. bring the plans up to date
    B. make corrections in the plans and specifications that will avoid future claims
    C. be certain that all bidders have the same information when bidding
    D. clarify the contract so as to keep the bid price down

8.____

9. A superintendent representing the contracting agency sees a worker performing an operation in an extremely hazardous and dangerous manner.
Of the following, the FIRST thing the superintendent should do is

    A. stop the man
    B. notify the shop steward
    C. notify the subcontractor's superintendent
    D. record the information in the Daily Log

9.____

10. Sometimes payments due a contractor are delayed in processing.
This situation is considered

    A. *good,* because the city saves interest on the money
    B. *poor,* because contractors will bid higher in the future to cover added financing costs
    C. *good,* because it pressures the contractor to complete the work faster
    D. *poor,* because the contractor may sue for his money

10.____

11. Of the following certificates required in the city during construction of a project, the one USUALLY required FIRST is a

    A. fuel oil storage certificate
    B. certificate of insurance
    C. fire department certificate
    D. certificate of occupancy

11.____

12. A license to install oil burners in the city is issued by the

    A. Department of Licenses   B. Fire Department
    C. Building Department   D. Civil Service Commission

12.____

13. The superintendent should instruct his concrete inspector that, when high-early strength cement is used and air temperatures are above 50°F, the EARLIEST time after pouring that concrete forms may be stripped is _____ hours.

   A. 24   B. 60   C. 72   D. 96

13.____

14. When a project superintendent is being transferred to another job, he should prepare a report about the job he is leaving.
Of the following, the MOST important item to be included in this report is a

   A. list of agency personnel and their duties on the job site
   B. list of all contractors and subcontractors on the job site
   C. statement of the status of the job and the unfinished work
   D. statement of new change orders

14.____

15. A contract contains a time penalty clause. There is a labor strike that stops construction for a month.
As a result, the contract completion date should

   A. remain as written
   B. be extended for one month
   C. be extended for two months
   D. be extended for the amount of time requested by the contractor

15.____

16. The MOST effective approach a project superintendent can take when he is dissatisfied with a contractor's work is to

   A. threaten to have the contractor replaced
   B. demand that the contractor replace his key men
   C. discuss withholding payment for the work with the contractor
   D. threaten to stop the job

16.____

17. To insure that the brick walls will be as specified, a sample brick panel is constructed.
The approval of this panel is PRIMARILY the responsibility of

   A. a superintendent representing the contracting agency
   B. an inspection firm representing the contracting agency
   C. an architect representing the contracting agency
   D. the supplier of the brick

17.____

18. In the standard operating procedures is the statement: A displacement of reinforcing bars of 1/2 inch might be of NO consequence in a foundation but might seriously weaken a thin slab.
Of the following, the BEST lesson to be learned from the above statement is:

   A. Inspection of foundations is not important
   B. Reinforcing steel in foundations does not have to be inspected
   C. foundations are less important than floor slabs
   D. Good judgment is required when inspecting construction

18.____

19. The standard operating procedures state: Preferably any deviation from the exact values specified should be in the direction of added quality.
An example of this dictum would be:

19.____

A. A concrete member should be made too thick rather than too thin
B. Air entrainment in concrete greater than that specified is desirable
C. The bottoms of footings should be made too high rather than too low
D. The greater the slump, the better the concrete

20. Of the following, the MOST important reason why the project superintendent represent- 20.____
    ing the contracting agency should keep a daily construction report form is that it

    A. is an important legal document used in resolving disputes
    B. enables the main office to keep tabs on the project superintendent
    C. enables the project superintendent to keep a permanent record of attendance of
       the inspectors under his jurisdiction
    D. enables the project superintendent to check on the payment requests from the
       contractor

21. In erecting structural steel, it was discovered that, in one connection of a beam to a col- 21.____
    umn, two holes in the connection angles did not have corresponding holes in the column.
    Of the following, the procedure to follow to resolve this problem is to

    A. burn the holes in the column in the field
    B. drill the holes in the column in the field
    C. have the column removed and sent to the shop to have the holes punched
    D. put a plug weld in the two holes

22. A general superintendent for the contracting agency visits the job site and tells the super- 22.____
    intendent of construction under his supervision that the workmanship on the exterior
    brickwork is sub-standard.
    Of the following, the BEST action for the superintendent of construction to take is to

    A. tell the general superintendent that he will give this phase of the work closer scru-
       tiny
    B. request that the specifications be made more specific
    C. recommend that the brick contractor be replaced
    D. ask the brick contractor to bring in a new crew of men or replace his foreman

23. An example of *non-destructive* testing is 23.____

    A. taking core borings in concrete
    B. x-raying a weld
    C. breaking concrete cylinders after 28 days
    D. checking the design of a structural element whose material is below specified
       strength

24. Of the following, the reference you should use to determine whether a sidewalk shed is 24.____
    required during the construction of a new school building is the

    A. standard specifications for the job
    B. building code
    C. OSHA standards
    D. standard details for the job

25. A superintendent of construction representing the contracting agency at the first job meeting tells the subcontractors and general contractor that if any of them tries to *pull a fast one* on him he will have them thrown off the job.
This action is

    A. *good,* because it will keep the contractors honest
    B. *good,* because they will not try to bypass the superintendent
    C. *poor,* because he cannot make good on his threat
    D. *poor,* because the contractors will retaliate against the superintendent

25.____

KEY (CORRECT ANSWERS)

1.	A		11.	B
2.	D		12.	C
3.	A		13.	A
4.	C		14.	C
5.	D		15.	B
6.	A		16.	C
7.	D		17.	C
8.	C		18.	D
9.	A		19.	A
10.	B		20.	A

21.	B
22.	A
23.	B
24.	B
25.	C

EXAMINATION SECTION
TEST 1

DIRECTIONS: Each question or incomplete statement is followed by several suggested answers or completions. Select the one that BEST answers the question or completes the statement. *PRINT THE LETTER OF THE CORRECT ANSWER IN THE SPACE AT THE RIGHT.*

QUESTIONS 1-16.

Questions 1 to 16, inclusive, refer to the drawings appearing on page 2.

1.   The structural support of the flooring is provided by   1.____

    A.   a concrete slab   B.   timber joists
    C.   steel beams   D.   piles

2.   The floor area of the plan and conference room measures, most nearly   2.____

    A.   18' x 28'   B.   21' x 30'
    C.   15' x 30'   D.   17' x 22'

3.   The *TOTAL* number of windows in the building is   3.____

    A.   12   B.   11   C.   10   D.   9

4.   The *CORRECT* number of coats of plaster required for this building is   4.____

    A.   0   B.   1   C.   2   D.   3

5.   The number of doors that measure 2'8" wide is   5.____

    A.   1   B.   2   C.   3   D.   4

6.   The number of convenience outlets in the superintendent's office is   6.____

    A.   0   B.   1   C.   2   D.   3

7.   The thickness of the partitions is, in inches, most nearly,   7.____

    A.   1 1/2   B.   2   C.   4   D.   6

8.   On the plan, just inside the entrance, is a notation 0'-0". This *MOST LIKELY* represents   8.____

    A.   the tolerance for the width of the door
    B.   the elevation above or below the floor
    C.   information relative to the radiator
    D.   information relative to the desk

9.   The height from floor to ceiling in the superintendent's office is, most nearly,   9.____

    A.   8' 0"   B.   9' 0"   C.   7' 0"   D.   8' 6"

10.   The height of the tops of the windows from the floor in the inspector's room is, most nearly,   10.____

    A.   6' 0"   B.   8' 0"   C.   7' 6"   D.   7' 0"

11.   The height of the floor above the ground is, most nearly,   11.____

    A.   6' 0"   B.   4' 8"   C.   3' 4"   D.   2' 8"

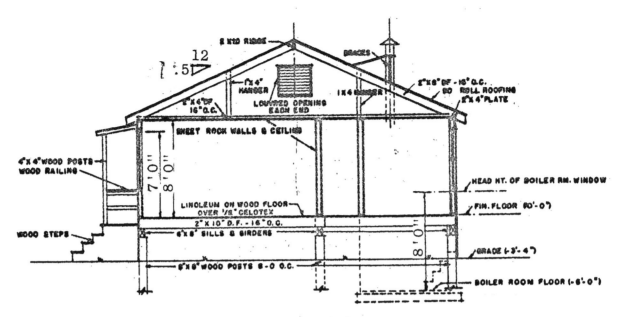

SECTION A-A

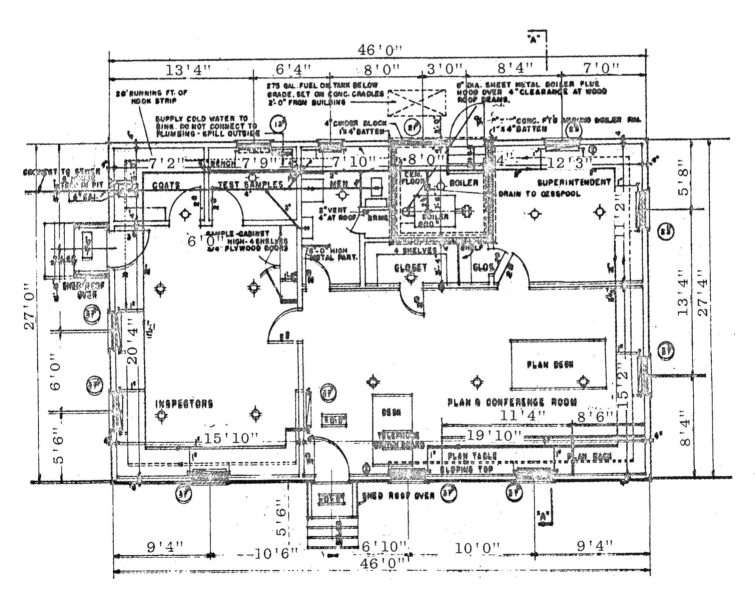

PLAN

12. Section A-A shows 8" x 8" wood posts supporting the sills and girders. The number of such posts required is, most nearly,   12.____

    A. 7   B. 14   C. 21   D. 28

13. Assume the roof rafters extend 1' 0" beyond the outside of the wall. The length of each rafter measures, most nearly,   13.____

    A. 14' 8"   B. 13' 8"   C. 16' 11"   D. 15' 11"

14. The wearing surface on the floor is to be   14.____

    A. linoleum   B. hardwood   C. celotex   D. asphalt tile

15. Referring to the stairway entrance to the building, if the treads are 10" each, then the distance from the edge of the landing to the entrance measures, most nearly,   15.____

    A. 2' 6"   B. 3' 0"   C. 3' 6"   D. 4' 0"

16. From the information shown on the plan and section, the height of each riser in the stairway measures, most nearly,   16.____

    A. 10"   B. 7 1/2"   C. 8"   D. 9"

17. The document known as the invitation to bidders does NOT have to include   17.____

    A. a description of the job
    B. the location of the job
    C. the plans and specifications for the job
    D. the name and address of the agency to which the bids are to be sent

18. The type of contract generally used on housing or school projects is   18.____

    A. unit price   B. cost plus
    C. fixed fee   D. lump sum

19. A lump-sum type of contract may require the contractor to submit a schedule of unit prices. Of the following, the BEST reason for this is that it   19.____

    A. prevents the lump sum from being too high
    B. provides a means of making equitable partial payments
    C. enables the estimators to check the total cost
    D. simplifies the selection of the lowest bidder

20. Instructions to bidders for a city housing project may require a bidder to submit a form of non-collusive affidavit.
The purpose of this is to   20.____

    A. bind the contractor to comply with the specifications
    B. obtain an honest bid
    C. make the contractor responsible for collusion with sub-contractors
    D. prevent a contractor from subletting the contract at a lower cost

QUESTIONS 21-23.

    The following specification refers to questions 21 to 23, inclusive:
    The minimum time of mixing shall be one minute per cubic yard after all the material, including the water, has been placed in the drum, and the drum shall be reversed for an additional two minutes. Mixing water shall be added only in the presence of the inspector.

21. From the above specifications, it is *REASONABLE* to conclude that   21.____

    A. the total mixing time of all the material, including the water, shall be at least 3 minutes for a one-yard batch
    B. the total mixing time of all the material, including the water, shall not be more than 3 minutes
    C. after the material has been mixed for 1 minute, the drum should be discharged and reversed for 2 minutes
    D. the material is mixed for one minute, the water is then added, and mixing continues for 2 more minutes

22. The above specification requires the presence of the inspector at the time the mixing water is added. The *PRIMARY* reason for this is that he should   22.____

    A. see the permit from the water department
    B. obtain the truck number
    C. check the amount of water added
    D. check the quality of water added

23. The above specification *MOST LIKELY* refers to   23.____

    A. transit mix concrete
    B. mortar for brick masonry
    C. plaster for scratch coat
    D. plaster for finish coat

QUESTIONS 24-25.

The following specification applies to questions 24 and 25:
Rough grading shall consist of cutting or filling to the elevation herein established with a permissible tolerance of two inches plus or minus. This tolerance shall be so used that, within any area of 100 feet, it will not be necessary for a later contractor performing fine grading to remove excess or bring additional fill to meet the required elevations.

24. From the above specification, it is *REASONABLE* to conclude that   24.____

    A. the total amount of excavation removed in rough grading should equal the total volume of excavation needed to meet the required elevations
    B. rough grading may end at an elevation 2 inches too high over an area 100' x 100'
    C. rough grading may end at an elevation 2 inches too low over an area 100' x 100'
    D. the contractor performing fine grading will not be permitted to remove excess material

25. Of the following, the BEST reason for specifying the above paragraph is that   25.____

    A. a stronger foundation is assured
    B. a savings in concrete will result
    C. by keeping above the water table a dry foundation is assured
    D. it establishes limits for the rough grading contractor

QUESTIONS 26-28.

The following specification applies to questions 26 to 28 inclusive:

All present walls, cellar floors, foundations, footings, and other existing structural items shall be removed as follows: Within 3 feet of all new building walls, areas and ramp walls, the above work shall be removed to the depth of new construction. Under new footings the above work shall be entirely removed.

26. From the above specification, it is *REASONABLE* to conclude that   26._____

    A.   present walls must be entirely removed if they are located directly under new walls
    B.   old footings may be left in place if they are located within three feet of new building walls
    C.   an existing foundation must be conpletely removed if located under a new footing
    D.   the depth of construction may reach a maximum within 3 feet of new walls

27. The above specification *MOST LIKELY* refers to removal of   27._____

    A.   walls and footings that were located off line
    B.   walls and footings located at incorrect grade
    C.   walls and footings of demolished buildings
    D.   defective foundations as determined by test

28. Of the following titles, the one that is *MOST* appropriate for the section in which the above specification appears is: 28._____

    A.   Work Not in Contract
    B.   Removal of City Property
    C.   Protection of Excavation
    D.   Preparation of Site

QUESTIONS 29-30.

The following specification applies to questions 29 and 30:
All exterior concrete exposed to view and interior walls in rooms to be finished shall be formed of plywood, composition, or steel forms. Finish of remainder may be equivalent to that obtained by use of matched 6-inch roofers.

29. From the above specification, it is *REASONABLE* to conclude that   29._____

    A.   matched 6-inch roofers give a better finish than composition or steel forms
    B.   interiors of exterior walls that are to be finished need not be carefully formed
    C.   formwork made up of 6-inch roofers may cause honeycombing
    D.   exterior concrete exposed to view should be more
    E.   carefully formed than other exterior concrete

30. The above specification is *MOST LIKELY* to be found in a section of the specifications titled: 30._____

    A.   Forms and Finish
    B.   Exterior Concrete
    C.   Unfinished Concrete Surfaces
    D.   Reinforcement for Concrete

31. If an acid wash is used on a new concrete surface, it will, *MOST LIKELY*,   31._____

    A. glaze the surface
    B. harden the surface
    C. make the surface soft and spongy
    D. disintegrate the surface

32. Of the following admixtures, the one that is *MOST LIKELY* to speed the setting of con-   32._____
crete is

    A. lamp black   B. calcium chloride
    C. hydrated lime   D. fly ash

33. The specifications state: Coarse aggregate shall consist of clean hard gravel or crushed   33._____
stone and shall be graded from 1/8 inch to 3/8 inch with not less than 95% passing a 3/8
inch mesh sieve and not more than 10% passing a No. 8 sieve.
Of the following, the coarse aggregate that would NOT meet the above specification is:

    A. All of the aggregate is between 1/8 inch and 3/8 inch in size
    B. 50% of the aggregate is 1/8 inch in diameter
    C. 5% of the aggregate is sand
    D. 15% of the aggregate is 1/2 inch in diameter

34. In the concrete for reinforced concrete, coarse agg-regate greater than a specified size is   34._____
not permitted *PRIMARILY* because

    A. it is more economical since less water is required in the mix
    B. large sized coarse aggregate may not pass between the reinforced bars
    C. smaller sized coarse aggregate makes a denser concrete
    D. this makes a lighter concrete

35. The specification for formwork for concrete states: Formwork for all slabs shall be set   35._____
with a camber of 1/4 inch for each 10 ft. of span.
The BEST reason for this is that the

    A. underside of the finished slab will be level
    B. formwork will have additional strength to resist construction stresses
    C. concrete will flow more easily into the forms
    D. bracing normally required to support the wood formwork will be eliminated

36. Cinder concrete is useful in building construction *PRIMARILY* because of its   36._____

    A. high density   B. imperviousness
    C. frost resistance   D. light weight

37. A tie bar in a cavity wall has a crimp in the center   37._____

     . The purpose of the crimp is to

    A. make the bar more rigid
    B. prevent water from passing across the bar
    C. provide a better bond in the masonry
    D. provide a means of hanging a board to catch surplus mortar

38. Cored brick may sometimes be specified for use as face brick. The minimum thickness between the core and the face of the brick *SHALL NOT BE LESS THAN*   38._____

    A. 1/4"   B. 3/8"   C. 1/2"   D. 3/4"

39. Assume the specifications allow the substitution of sand-lime brick for common brick in certain locations. Of the following, the location at which it is LEAST likely that such substitution would be permitted is   39._____

    A. backing-up   B. chimney flues
    C. piers   D. walls

40. Of the following, the *ONE* that may *MOST LIKELY* be the cause of map cracking in the finish coat of plaster is   40._____

    A. a weak brown coat
    B. too much moisture present
    C. a warm dry draft blowing on fresh plaster
    D. too much retarder in the mix

41. An inspector reports a dryout in a room that has just been plastered. The MOST appropriate course of action to take is to   41._____

    A. wait until the plaster sets and determine the extent of the damage
    B. order the dryout removed and replastered
    C. order an increase in the amount of retarder used in the mix
    D. allow the contractor to spray water on the dry spot so that setting action may start again

42. The temperature below which it is NOT good practice to do plastering is, in degrees F, most nearly,   42._____

    A. 72   B. 65   C. 50   D. 36

43. Gaging plaster that is used to accelerate the setting time of finish coat plaster is, generally,   43._____

    A. plaster of Paris   B. hydrated lime
    C. keene's cement   D. dolomitic lime

44. Where bond plaster is specified for the scratch coat, it is generally required that the bond plaster be   44._____

    A. mixed with lime putty
    B. mixed neat without the addition of sand
    C. slaked at least 24 hours before use
    D. mixed with gypsum gaging plaster

45. For the finish coat of a three-coat plaster job, it is *MOST LIKELY* that the specifications would call for   45._____

    A. vermiculite   B. silicon
    C. perlite   D. gypsum

46. Good practice in laying asphalt tile requires that the temperature of the room, in degrees F, be *NOT LESS THAN*   46.____

    A. 32   B. 50   C. 70   D. 80

47. The joints in 2" face wood flooring are *MOST LIKELY* to be   47.____

    A. mortise and tenon   B. tongue and groove
    C. butt   D. dove-tail

48. Of the following species of wood, the *ONE* that is *MOST LIKELY* to be specified for finish flooring in a school or housing project is   48.____

    A. Douglas Fir   B. Sitka Spruce
    C. Northern Hard Maple   D. Hickory

49. Of the following, the *ONE* that is *MOST LIKELY* to be specified for fastening wood flooring in concrete is   49.____

    A. dowels in the concrete
    B. sleepers in the concrete
    C. set flooring in fresh concrete
    D. spread thin layer of grout and set flooring therein

50. After asphalt tile is cemented in place, the specifications generally require that it shall be   50.____

    A. cleaned only   B. cleaned and waxed
    C. cleaned and stained   D. cleaned and shellacked

KEY (CORRECT ANSWERS)

1. B	11. C	21. A	31. D	41. D
2. C	12. C	22. C	32. B	42. C
3. B	13. D	23. A	33. D	43. A
4. A	14. A	24. A	34. B	44. B
5. D	15. B	25. D	35. A	45. D
6. B	16. C	26. C	36. D	46. C
7. C	17. C	27. C	37. B	47. B
8. B	18. D	28. D	38. D	48. C
9. A	19. B	29. D	39. B	49. B
10. D	20. B	30. A	40. A	50. A

EXAMINATION SECTION
TEST 1

DIRECTIONS: Each question or incomplete statement is followed by several suggested answers or completions. Select the one that BEST answers the question or completes the statement. *PRINT THE LETTER OF THE CORRECT ANSWER IN THE SPACE AT THE RIGHT.*

1. One reason for specifying back-puttying in glazed work is that

    A. it seals the window against air and rain leaks
    B. less putty is required in this method
    C. the use of glazing clips is not required
    D. it is easier to apply putty on the inside of the glass than on the outside

1.____

2. A specification on finished hardware refers to Roses and Escutcheon plates. These are *MOST LIKELY* to be installed on

    A. desks   B. blackboards   C. windows   D. doors

2.____

3. Of the following statements, the one that *MOST CLOSELY* identifies the term "house sewer" is: The house sewer is

    A. located outside the building area and connects to the public sewer in the street
    B. located inside the building area and ends at the outside of the front wall of the building
    C. the pipe which carries the discharge from the plumbing fixtures to the house drain
    D. the house drain

3.____

4. A concrete level roof is to receive 4-ply composition slag roofing with insulation. The *FIRST* item to cover the concrete is

    A. the insulation   B. the slag
    C. a layer of felt   D. a bed of hot pitch

4.____

5. A common example of a paint thinner is usually

    A. tung oil   B. chinawood oil
    C. lead oxide   D. turpentine

5.____

6. In the painting of rooms in a housing project or school by the contractor, the superintendent representing the city is LEAST concerned with

    A. the area covered per man per day
    B. whether the paint is being used at the required spreading rate
    C. the moisture content of the plaster
    D. the condition of the surfaces to be painted

6.____

QUESTIONS 7-9.

Questions 7 to 9, inclusive, refer to the diagram shown below:

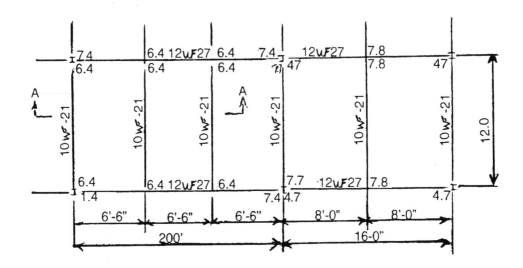

FLOOR PLAN

TOP OF BEAM 3 1/2" BELOW FINISHED FLOOR LEVEL

LIVE LOAD = 100#/SQ.FT.

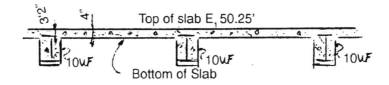

SECTION A-A

7. The elevation of the underside of the 4" slab is most nearly,   7._____

    A. 49.92   B. 50.00   C. 50.12   D. 50.25

8. The figures such as 6.4 and 4.7 represent, most nearly, the   8._____

    A. deadweight reactions of the slab
    B. distances to the points of 0 shear
    C. maximum moments that the beams carry
    D. end reactions of the beams

9. Of the following, the BEST reason for encasing the steel beams in concrete is to   9._____

    A. increase their resistance to corrosion
    B. simplify the formwork
    C. increase the deadweight of the floor
    D. increase their fire resistance

10. Splices in the steel columns of a tall steel frame building are usually located approxi-   10._____
mately

    A. 2' above the floor
    B. 2' below the floor

C. halfway between floors
D. at the level the floor beams frame into the column

11. Rivets that are to be driven in the field are usually heated until the color is   11.____

A. white   B. light blue   C. cherry red   D. dull black

12. Reinforcing steel is *USUALLY* bent to its final shape   12.____

A. on the jobsite   B. at the mill
C. at the warehouse   D. in the shop

13. Copper sheet is *USUALLY* specified   13.____

A. Birmingham Gage   B. United States Steel Gage
C. in ounces per square foot   D. in pounds per square yard

14. The thickness of a 16-gage plate is, in inches, most nearly,   14.____

A. 1/16   B. 1/8   C. 3/16   D. 1/4

15. A loose lintel is a lintel that   15.____

A. has less than 4 inches of bearing on the masonry
B. is not connected to the structural steel work
C. is used over doors but not over windows
D. should have a minimum bearing of 8" on the surface on which it rests

16. The diameter of a #6 reinforcing bar is, in inches, most nearly,   16.____

A. 3/8   B. 1/2   C. 5/8   D. 3/4

17. The bent bar marked "A" is *USUALLY* called a   17.____

A. tylag
B. government anchor
C. dead man
D. strap bar

18. "Legal Curb Level", according to the code, means, most nearly,   18.____

A. the curb level established by the county
B. the curb level established by the department of public works
C. that it is 6" above the crown of the road
D. that it is the elevation established by the law department of the city

19. Of the following soils, the *ONE* that is *MOST* compressible is usually   19.____

A. hardpan   B. sand   C. gravel   D. clay

20. The specifications state: Excavated material shall only be considered as rock when the Superintendent agrees that because of its density the most practical and economical method of removing same is by means of explosives. When rock is disintegrated to such an extent that it can readily be loosened by steam shovels or manually by tools not requiring fuel or power, then such material shall be regarded as earth excavation. Referring to the specification above, the *MOST NEARLY* correct statement is:

    A. A cubic yard boulder is considered rock excavation
    B. Material that can be economically removed only by explosives shall be classified as rock
    C. All disintegrated rock is to be classified under earth excavation
    D. If any material requires a steam shovel for its removal, it shall be classified as rock

20.____

21. Of the following, the *ONE* that is of LEAST importance to the inspector on timber pile driving is the

    A. plumbing of mandrel befroe driving
    B. condition of the pile before driving
    C. plumbness of pile
    D. final position of the pile

21.____

22. Of the following, the *MOST* important advantage in the use of steel shell piles is the

    A. savings in concrete
    B. opportunity for better inspection
    C. simplified pile cap construction
    D. elimination of pile caps

22.____

23. The Engineering News-Record formula for piles is $P = \dfrac{2\,Wh}{s + c}$

The letter s represents, *MOST NEARLY,* the

    A. factor of safety used
    B. number of the hammer used
    C. average penetration of the last 5 blows in inches
    D. distance the pile has travelled vertically in feet

23.____

24. In the Engineering News-Record formula, the term "Wh" represents, *MOST NEARLY,* the

    A. weight of pile multiplied by height of hammer falls
    B. bearing energy of the pile
    C. weight of hammer multiplied by the height of fall
    D. speed at which the pile goes inth the ground

24.____

25. In the Engineering News-Record formula, the term c represents, *MOST NEARLY,*

    A. a constant depending upon the type of hammer used
    B. a correction factor that corrects for rebound
    C. the factor that allows a suitable factor of safety
    D. the penetration caused by the last blow

25.____

26. If steel weighs 490 #/cu. ft., the weight of a 1-inch square steel bar 1 foot long is, in pounds, *MOST NEARLY,*   26.____

    A. .434   B. 3.4   C. 42   D. 49

27. The invert elevation of a sewer is 18.54 at Manhole 1 and 18.22 at Manhole 2, 250 feet from Manhole 1. The slope of the sewer per foot is, *MOST NEARLY,*   27.____

    A. .0013   B. .32   C. .01   D. 0.1

QUESTIONS 28-31.
    Questions 28 to 31, inclusive, refer to the diagram shown below.

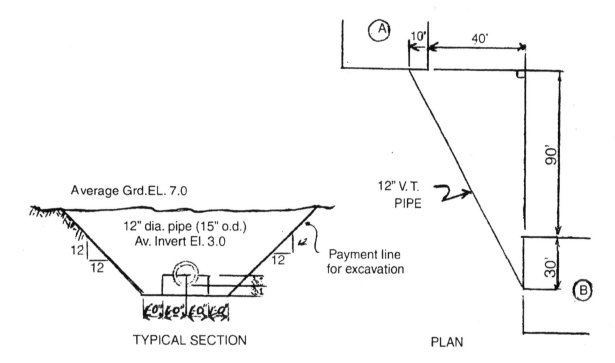

TYPICAL SECTION   PLAN

28. The length of the 12" vitrified pipe between Building A and Building B is, in feet, *MOST NEARLY,*   28.____

    A. 120   B. 130   C. 140   D. 150

29. For 100 feet of pipe, the volume of concrete in the concrete cradle under the pipe, is, in cubic yards, *MOST NEARLY,*   29.____

    A. 5.0   B. 6.0   C. 7.0   D. 9.0

30. The volume of payment excavation for 100 feet of trench is, in cubic yards, *MOST NEARLY,*   30.____

    A. 95   B. 120   C. 140   D. 165

31. The method of excavation shown in the typical section is *USUALLY* called   31.____

    A. skeleton sheeted   B. open cut
    C. lined   D. wellpointed

32. Shown below is a section through a concrete retaining wall. The volume of concrete per foot of retaining wall is, in cubic feet, *MOST NEARLY,*

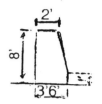

    A. 23.2
    B. 25.0
    C. 26.8
    D. 28.8

QUESTIONS 33-39.

    Questions 33 to 39, inclusive, refer to the diagram shown below.

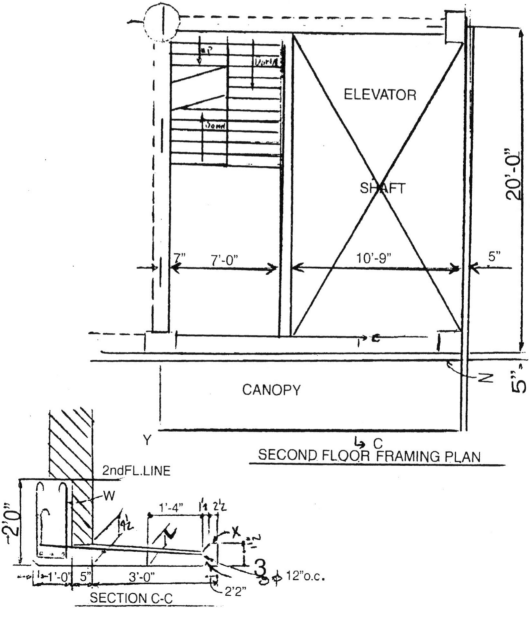

SECOND FLOOR FRAMING PLAN

SECTION C-C

33. The elevation of the top of the outer edge of the canopy marked "X" is, *MOST NEARLY,*

    A. 20.46   B. 20.42   C. 20.38   D. 20.34

34. The triangular inset on the bottom of the canopy marked "Y" is *USUALLY* called a   34.____

    A. raggle   B. reglet   C. drip   D. setback

35. Assuming the reinforcing steel is to be stopped 3 inches from the edge of the concrete   35.____
and the bars marked 3/8" round at 12" o.c. are straight bars, the ordered length of the
above mentioned bars should be, *MOST NEARLY,*

    A. 3' 11"   B. 19' 6"   C. 18' 6"   D. 19' 0"

36. In the plan, the line marked "Z" is the   36.____

    A. outside face of the canopy
    B. outside face of the masonry wall
    C. inside face of the reinforced concrete beam
    D. outside face of the reinforced concrete beam

37. The canopy is considered   37.____

    A. pre-stressed concrete
    B. a simply supported beam
    C. a cantilever
    D. pre-cast concrete

38. The bar marked "W" is usually called a   38.____

    A. chair   B. tie bar   C. stirrup   D. spacer

39. The dimension "V" is, in inches, *MOST NEARLY,*   39.____

    A. 4 1/8   B. 4 1/4   C. 4 3/8   D. 4 1/2

40. Of the following, the BEST way to measure a distance on a map with a scale of 1" =20' is   40.____
to use a(n)

    A. planimeter set to the correct scale
    B. 50 foot tape
    C. engineer's scale
    D. architect's scale

41. The following appears on a floor plan The _____ 3'0" _____   41.____
3'0" *MOST LIKELY* represents a

    A. double acting door 3'0" wide
    B. fire door
    C. door, 3'0" wide
    D. masonry opening, 3'0" wide

42. The following symbol on a plumbing plan   42.____
MOST LIKELY represents a

    A. check valve
    B. vent
    C. sump
    D. trap

43. In the wall section shown below, the dimension that would *MOST LIKELY* represent the story height is   43.____

    A. A
    B. B
    C. C
    D. D

44. According to the section shown in the previous problem, the type of floor construction is, *MOST LIKELY,*   44.____

    A. reinforced concrete
    B. timber joist and wood flooring
    C. steel joist and wood flooring
    D. steel joist and cement flooring

45. A fixed amount of money is held from the contractor for a period of a year after the completion of construction. The BEST reason for this is   45.____

    A. that it acts as a security for the repair of defective work after completion of the construction
    B. to penalize the contractor for poor work
    C. the money will be available for modifications in the design of the structure
    D. the money will be available for taxes due

46. A "punch list" is usually a list   46.____

    A. showing the checkoff of union dues
    B. showing inspector's attendance
    C. of defects requiring correction by the contractor
    D. of injuries to the contractor's personnel kept for purpose of protecting the city against suit

47. The part of the structure that is *MOST LIKELY* to be affected by unforeseen existing conditions is the   47.____

    A. steel framework   B. plumbing
    C. electrical   D. foundation

48. The specifications state that no live load be placed on a concrete structure immediately following the stripping of its formwork.
The BEST reason for this is   48.____

    A. the design of the structure may be wrong
    B. the concrete will not cure properly

C. to allow the easy removal of the formwork
D. to prevent overstressing of the concrete

49. A superintendent should have sufficient confidence in himself and his judgment to take a   49._____
positive stand when the occasion arises and requires it. A man who changes his mind
frequently, reversing his rulings under pressure, does not belong in such a position. However, if he has made a mistake, he should not be obstinate and refuse to alter his position. But too many such mistakes will demonstrate that he is unfit for the job.
From the above statement, it is *REASONABLE* to conclude that a

A. superintendent should stick to his decision, right or wrong
B. good superintendent will never make mistakes
C. superintendent should not be so bull-headed as to refuse to back down where he is
    manifestly wrong
D. man who changes his mind frequently is merely trying to avoid mistakes

50. Assume that a contractor disagrees with a ruling of the general superintendent and you,   50._____
as a superintendent, believe the contractor is correct. You should

A. tell him to disregard the ruling until you discuss it with the general superintendent
B. tell him to stop talking about it since the general superintendent is not going to
    change his mind
C. ignore the criticism on the theory that the contractor will oppose any ruling of the
    general superintendent
D. tell him you will bring his criticism to the attention of the general superintendent

_____

KEY (CORRECT ANSWERS)

1.	A	11.	C	21.	A	31.	B	41.	C
2.	D	12.	A	22.	B	32.	A	42.	D
3.	A	13.	C	23.	C	33.	A	43.	B
4.	D	14.	A	24.	C	34.	C	44.	A
5.	D	15.	B	25.	A	35.	C	45.	A
6.	A	16.	D	26.	B	36.	B	46.	C
7.	A	17.	B	27.	A	37.	C	47.	D
8.	D	18.	A	28.	B	38.	C	48.	D
9.	D	19.	D	29.	A	39.	B	49.	C
10.	A	20.	B	30.	C	40.	C	50.	D

_____

EXAMINATION SECTION
TEST 1

DIRECTIONS: Each question or incomplete statement is followed by several suggested answers or completions. Select the one that BEST answers the question or completes the statement. *PRINT THE LETTER OF THE CORRECT ANSWER IN THE SPACE AT THE RIGHT.*

1. Of the following, the BEST reason for using vibrators in concrete construction is to   1.____

    A. remove excess water
    B. consolidate the concrete
    C. increase the slump of the concrete
    D. retard the setting of the concrete

2. When a contractor fails to adhere to an approved progress schedule, he should   2.____

    A. revise the schedule without delay
    B. ask for an extension of time on account of delays
    C. adopt such additional means and methods of construction as will make up for the time lost
    D. take no immediate action with the hope that sufficient time will be available later on that will assure the completion in accordance with the schedule

3. The usual contract for work includes a section entitled *Instructions to Bidders* which states that the   3.____

    A. contractor agrees that he has made his own examination and will make no claim for damages on account of errors or omissions
    B. contractor shall not make claims for damages of any discrepancy, error, or omission in any plans
    C. estimates of quantities and calculations are guaranteed by the board to be correct and are deemed to be a representation of the conditions affecting the work
    D. plans, measurements, dimensions, and conditions under which the work is to be performed are guaranteed by the board

4. Specifications covering brickwork usually require special precautions and protection for work in cold weather.   4.____
The HIGHEST temperature below which these measures are required is *most nearly*

    A. 50° F   B. 40° F   C. 30° F   D. 20° F

5. Controlled concrete is required for the reinforced concrete frame of a large school building. The ultimate strength of this concrete will be *most nearly* _____ pounds per square inch.   5.____

    A. 1000   B. 3000   C. 5000   D. 7000

6. A lump sum type of contract may require the contractor to submit a schedule of unit prices.   6.____
The BEST reason for this is that it

    A. prevents the lump sum from being too high
    B. simplifies the selection of the lowest bidder

C. enables the estimators to check the total cost
D. provides a means of making equitable partial payments

7. The concrete test that will BEST determine the consistency of a concrete mix is the   7._____

   A. slump test   B. sieve analysis
   C. calorimetric test   D. water-cement ratio test

8. The BEST way to evaluate the overall state of completion of a construction project is to   8._____
check the progress estimate against the

   A. inspection work sheet
   B. construction schedule
   C. inspector's checklist
   D. equipment maintenance schedule

Questions 9-15.

DIRECTIONS: Questions 9 through 15 refer to the sketch below.

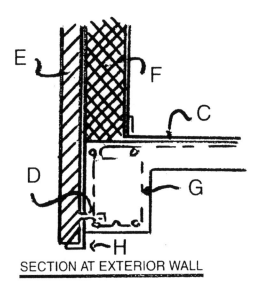

SECTION AT EXTERIOR WALL

9. The floor is made of   9._____

   A. air-entrained concrete
   B. reinforced concrete
   C. lightweight concrete
   D. concrete-encased structural steel

10. The exterior wall is a _____ wall.   10._____

   A. concrete block   B. cavity construction
   C. veneer   D. solid brick

11. Member C is a   11._____

   A. deformed bar   B. hooked bar
   C. plain bar   D. shear connector

12. Member E is made of   12.____

    A. steel   B. wood   C. brick   D. concrete

13. Member F is   13.____

    A. concrete block   B. facing brick
    C. glazed tile   D. sheetrock

14. Member G is a   14.____

    A. longitudinal bar   B. splice
    C. stirrup   D. tie wire

15. Member H is a   15.____

    A. purlin   B. brace   C. guy   D. lintel

16. A projected sash is a(n)   16.____

    A. architectural projection from a building exterior which breaks up a smooth pattern of the wall
    B. double-hung window
    C. window that opens inward or outward
    D. window that has a screen attachment

17. In the construction of cellar concrete floors resting on earth, the item that should be checked MOST carefully is that   17.____

    A. the earth is wet before pouring
    B. all backfill is granular soil
    C. the earth is dry before pouring
    D. all backfill is properly compacted

18. Specifications state that column dowels are embedded 24 diameters in the footing. The length of embedment for a number 6 bar is _____ inches.   18.____

    A. 6   B. 12   C. 18   D. 24

19. After excavating to the subgrade of a footing, an examination of the soil reveals that it is of a poorer quality than the soil in that area and at that elevation shown on the soil borings.
Of the following types of footings, the one that would be LEAST affected by this condition is a   19.____

    A. footing on piles   B. plain concrete footing
    C. combined footing   D. spread footing

20. The MAIN reason for requiring written job reports is to   20.____

    A. avoid the necessity of oral orders
    B. develop better methods of doing the work
    C. provide a permanent record of what was done
    D. increase the amount of work that can be done

21. Of the following items, the one which should NOT be included in a proposed work schedule is   21.____

    A. a schedule of hourly wage rates and supplementary benefits
    B. an estimated time required for delivery of materials and equipment
    C. the anticipated commencement and completion of the various operations
    D. the sequence and inter-relationship of various operations with those of related contracts

22. A specification requires that brick be laid with *shoved* joints. The BEST reason for this requirement is that it helps the bricklayer to obtain _____ joint(s).   22.____

    A. full
    B. plumb vertical
    C. level horizontal
    D. the required thickness of

23. A specification states that access panels to suspended ceilings will be of metal. The MAIN reason for providing access panels is to   23.____

    A. improve the insulation of the ceiling
    B. improve the appearance of the ceiling
    C. make it easier to construct the building
    D. make it easier to maintain the building

24. A three-coat plaster job is to be 7/8 inches thick. Of the following, the thickness of the individual coats, in inches, would be *most nearly* scratch   24.____

    A. 1/8, brown 1/2, finish 1/4
    B. 3/8, brown 3/8, finish 1/8
    C. 11/16, brown 1/8, finish 1/16
    D. 5/16, brown 1/4, finish 5/16

25. You are assigned to keep a record of the number and volume of all boulders excavated that exceed one cubic yard in volume.
The MOST probable reason for this order is: 25.____

    A. Any delays in excavating due to the boulders may result in a claim
    B. The contractor may receive additional payment for rock excavation
    C. There may be an extra charge for hauling boulders from the jobsite
    D. Excavation where there are large boulders involved is dangerous, and in the event of an accident, you will have appropriate records

KEY (CORRECT ANSWERS)

1. B	11. B
2. C	12. C
3. A	13. A
4. B	14. C
5. B	15. D
6. D	16. C
7. A	17. D
8. B	18. C
9. B	19. A
10. C	20. C

21. A
22. A
23. D
24. B
25. C

TEST 2

DIRECTIONS: Each question or incomplete statement is followed by several suggested answers or completions. Select the one that BEST answers the question or completes the statement. *PRINT THE LETTER OF THE CORRECT ANSWER IN THE SPACE AT THE RIGHT.*

1. Which one of the following is the PRIMARY object in drawing up a set of specifications for materials to be purchased?

   A. Control of quality
   B. Outline of intended use
   C. Establishment of standard sizes
   D. Location and method of inspection

   1.____

2. In order to avoid disputes over payments for extra work in a contract for construction, the BEST procedure to follow would be to

   A. have contractor submit work progress reports daily
   B. insert a special clause in the contract specifications
   C. have a representative on the job at all times to verify conditions
   D. allocate a certain percentage of the cost of the job to cover such expenses

   2.____

3. If there is a small amount of water on the surface of a newly-laid concrete sidewalk, the recommended procedure *before* finishing is to

   A. allow it to evaporate
   B. remove it with a broom
   C. sprinkle some dry cement on top
   D. remove it with a float

   3.____

4. Prior to the installation of equipment called for in the specifications, the contractor is *usually* required to submit for approval

   A. sets of shop drawings
   B. a set of revised specifications
   C. a detailed description of the methods of work to be used
   D. a complete list of skilled and unskilled tradesmen he proposes to use

   4.____

5. A specification on piles states that plumbness must be within 2% of the pile length. If the pile length is 30 feet, the MAXIMUM amount that the pile may be out of plumb is, in inches, *most nearly*

   A. 5   B. 6   C. 7   D. 8

   5.____

6. The number of days that it will take high early strength concrete to equal the 28-day strength of normal portland cement concrete is *most nearly*

   A. 1   B. 3   C. 7   D. 12

   6.____

7. Specifications may state that a standpipe system will be provided in each building. The MAIN purpose of a standpipe system is to

   A. supply the roof water tank
   B. provide water for firefighting

   7.____

C. circulate water for the heating system
D. provide adequate pressure for the water supply

8. The drawing which should be used as a legal reference when checking completed construction work is the _____ drawing.

    A. contract   B. assembly
    C. working or shop   D. preliminary

8.____

9. Efflorescence may BEST be removed from brickwork by washing with a solution of _____ acid.

    A. muriatic   B. citric   C. carbonic   D. nitric

9.____

10. The MAIN difference between sheet glass and plate glass is

    A. the surface finish of the two types of glass
    B. the heat absorbing qualities of the two types of glass
    C. plate glass is thinner than sheet glass
    D. plate glass is tempered while sheet glass is not tempered

10.____

11. Construction joints in the concrete columns of a multistory building are *usually* located

    A. at floor level
    B. 1 foot above floor level
    C. at the underside of floor slab
    D. at the underside of deepest beam framing into the column

11.____

12. A contractor on a large construction project *usually* receives partial payments based on

    A. estimates of completed work
    B. actual cost of materials delivered and work completed
    C. estimates of material delivered and not paid for by the contractor
    D. the breakdown estimate submitted after the contract was signed and prorated over the estimated duration of the contract

12.____

13. According to the building code, masonry footings shall extend at least 4' below finished grade.
The PRIMARY reason for this is to

    A. get below the frost line
    B. make the foundation stronger
    C. keep water out of the basement
    D. reach a lower soil strata where better bearing material can be found

13.____

14. Good inspection methods require that the inspector

    A. be observant and check all details
    B. constantly check with the engineer who designed the school
    C. apply specifications according to his interpretation
    D. permit slight job variation to establish good public relations

14.____

Questions 15-19.

DIRECTIONS: Questions 15 through 19 refer to the following specification for wood flooring. In answering these questions, refer to this specification.

2" x 4" wood sleepers laid flat @ 16" o.c.
1" x 6" sub flooring, laid diagonally; cut at butt joints with parallel cuts; joints at center of sleepers, well staggered, no two joints side by side. Not less than 1/8" space between boards.
One layer of 15# asphalt felt on top of sub-floor.
Finish floor - North Rock Maple, T & G, laid perpendicular to sleepers; 8d nails not more than 12" apart; end joints well scattered with at least 2 flooring strips between joints.
Flooring 25/32" x 2 1/4" face - 1st quality.

15.   It is *most likely* that the floor referred to in the specification is to be laid   15._____

     A.   directly on the ground   B.   on a concrete base
     C.   on wood joists   D.   on steel beams

16.   The BEST reason for specifying that the sub-flooring be parallel cut at butt joints is that   16._____
this

     A.   requires less material
     B.   provides staggered joints
     C.   provides more nailing surface
     D.   allows the joint to fall between sleepers

17.   The BEST reason for specifying a minimum space between the sub-floor boards is that it   17._____

     A.   saves on material   B.   reduces creaking
     C.   allows for expansion   D.   prevents dry rot

18.   The BEST reason for specifying at least 2 flooring strips between joints in the finish floor-   18._____
ing is that

     A.   it looks better
     B.   it is more economical
     C.   each board is supported by two adjoining boards
     D.   each finish board is supported by at least two sub-floor boards

19.   The BEST reason for placing asphalt felt on top of the sub-floor is to   19._____

     A.   deaden noise   B.   preserve the wood
     C.   reduce dampness   D.   permit movement

20.   Assume you are recommending in a report to your superior that a radical change in a   20._____
standard maintenance procedure should be adopted.
Of the following, the MOST important information to be included in this report is

     A.   a list of the reasons for making this change
     B.   the names of the other GSSM who favor the change
     C.   a complete description of the present procedure
     D.   amount of training time needed for the new procedure

21. Specifications require that the first floor beams of a building must be in place before backfill is placed against the foundation walls.
The BEST reason for this requirement is that

    A. without the first floor beams in place, the wall may become overstressed
    B. it is easier to inspect the first floor construction when the backfill is not in place
    C. the utilities up to the first floor level should be in place before backfill is placed
    D. the boiler setting hung from the first floor must be in place before backfill is placed

21.____

22. The frequency with which job reports are submitted should depend MAINLY on

    A. how comprehensive the report has to be
    B. the amount of information in the report
    C. the availability of an experienced man to write the report
    D. the importance of changes in the information included in the report

22.____

23. Assume that a contractor proposed to start the roofing three days after pouring the concrete roof slab.
This proposal is

    A. *good,* mainly since it will speed the construction
    B. *good,* mainly since it will assist in curing the concrete
    C. *poor* in cold weather but is all right in warm weather
    D. *poor,* mainly since excess water in the concrete may bulge the roofing

23.____

24. In performing field inspectional work, an inspector is the contact man between the public and the board, and it is his job to secure compliance through the maximum utilization of persuasion and education and the minimum application of coercion.
According to the above statement, an inspector performing inspectional duties should

    A. seek to obtain voluntary compliance and use coercion only as a last resort
    B. be conciliatory on all issues of non-compliance and not take an attitude of firmness and authority
    C. maintain a strictly impersonal attitude in the exercise of his duties at all times
    D. use the threat of legal action to secure conformance with specified requirements

24.____

25. A specification requires that brick should be thoroughly wet before using.
Of the following, the BEST reason for this requirement is that

    A. wetting the brick uncovers hidden flaws
    B. it is easier to shove wet brick into place
    C. wetting cleans the pores of the brick ensuring a stronger bond
    D. wetting decreases absorption of water from the mortar

25.____

KEY (CORRECT ANSWERS)

1.	A	11.	A
2.	C	12.	A
3.	A	13.	A
4.	A	14.	A
5.	C	15.	B
6.	C	16.	C
7.	B	17.	C
8.	A	18.	C
9.	A	19.	C
10.	A	20.	A

21.	A
22.	D
23.	D
24.	A
25.	D

TEST 3

DIRECTIONS: Each question or incomplete statement is followed by several suggested answers or completions. Select the one that BEST answers the question or completes the statement. *PRINT THE LETTER OF THE CORRECT ANSWER IN THE SPACE AT THE RIGHT.*

Questions 1-4.

DIRECTIONS: Questions 1 to 4 refer to the sketch below.

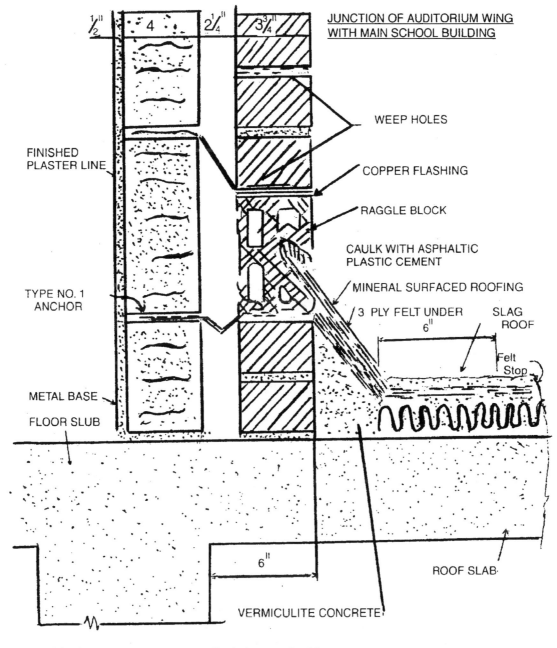

1.   The 1/2" of plaster would *most likely* be applied in _____ coats.   1.____

   A.   one   B.   two   C.   three   D.   four

2. Vermiculite concrete is PRIMARILY _____ concrete.　　　　　　　　2._____

   A.　low-slump
   C.　an air-entrained
   B.　water-resistant
   D.　a lightweight

3. Which of the following statements relating to copper flashing is CORRECT? It　　3._____

   A.　is perforated in the air space
   B.　consists of one solid continuous sheet
   C.　consists of 2-inch strips spaced every foot
   D.　is provided to prevent the fall of mortar into the air space

4. The 4-inch thick material is *most likely*　　　　　　　　　　　　　4._____

   A.　cinder block
   C.　brick
   B.　gypsum block
   D.　terra cotta

5. A rowlock course of brick is one in which the bricks are laid　　　　　　5._____

   A.　on their 2 1/4" x 8" surface
   B.　in an interlocking fashion
   C.　with dowels at set intervals
   D.　in a one-header followed by a one-stretcher course

6. Specifications for excavation for spread footings require that machine excavation be to　　6._____
   within a foot of the final subgrade and the remainder of the excavation shall be by hand.
   The BEST reason for this requirement is to

   A.　prevent cave-ins near the excavation
   B.　cut down on the amount of fill needed
   C.　prevent excavation below the subgrade
   D.　insure that the area in the vicinity of the footing not be excessively disturbed

7. The CHIEF purpose in preparing an outline for a report is *usually* to insure that　　7._____

   A.　the report will be grammatically correct
   B.　every point will be given equal emphasis
   C.　principal and secondary points will be properly integrated
   D.　the language of the report will be of the same level and include the same technical
   terms

8. One of the properties of tempered plate glass which affects installation is that it　　8._____

   A.　has a blue tinge
   B.　cannot be cut after the glass is tempered
   C.　does not bond with putty or glazing compound
   D.　cracks more easily than ordinary plate glass

9. In assigning the men to various jobs, the BEST principle for a supervisor to follow is to　　9._____

   A.　study the men's abilities and assign them accordingly
   B.　rotate a man from job to job until you find one which he can do well
   C.　assign each of them to a job and let them adjust to it in their own way
   D.　assume that men appointed to the position can do all parts of the work equally well

10. With respect to waterproofing existing basements, the MOST effective and lasting repairs   10.____
    are those made

    A. on the earth side of a basement wall
    B. on the inside basement wall surface
    C. on the floor
    D. in the mortar joints

11. During the actual construction work, the CHIEF value of a construction schedule is to   11.____

    A. insure that the work will be done on time
    B. reveal when production is behind schedule
    C. show how much equipment and material is required for the project
    D. furnish data as to the methods and techniques of construction operations

12. When building the formwork for a 12" doubly reinforced concrete wall, the USUAL order   12.____
    of construction is place the

    A. formwork for both faces of the wall; then place the reinforcing steel
    B. reinforcing steel and then place the formwork for both faces of the wall
    C. formwork for one face of the wall, place the reinforcing steel, and then place the
       formwork for the other face of the wall
    D. formwork for one face of the wall, place the reinforcing steel for one face, place the
       formwork for the other face of the wall, and then place the reinforcement for the
       second face

13. The GREATEST period of time must elapse between   13.____

    A. pouring and stripping concrete formwork
    B. placing reinforcing steel and pouring concrete
    C. applying the finish plaster coat and painting a plastered wall
    D. applying the first and second coats of a 3-coat plaster job for a wall

14. A fixed amount of money is generally withheld from the contractor for a definite period   14.____
    after the completion of construction.
    The BEST reason for this is

    A. that the money will be available for taxes due
    B. to penalize the contractor for poor work
    C. that it is a security for the repair of any defective work
    D. that the money will be available for modifications in the design of the structure

15. The practice of applying the brown coat to a wall on the day after the scratch coat of gyp-   15.____
    sum plaster was applied is GENERALLY considered

    A. satisfactory
    B. satisfactory only if the temperature is between 50° and 70° F
    C. unsatisfactory because 7 days must elapse between the application of the scratch
       and brown coats
    D. unsatisfactory because at least 3 days must elapse between the application of the
       scratch and brown coats

16. Fiberboard material 2 inches thick is placed on a flat reinforced concrete roof.   16._____
    The PRIMARY function of this 2 inch thick material is to

    A. act as a vapor barrier
    B. soundproof the rooms below
    C. prevent loss of heat from the building
    D. keep water from penetrating the ceiling below

17. The PRIMARY purpose of adding lime to a mortar mix is to   17._____

    A. improve the appearance of the mortar
    B. increase the workability of the mortar
    C. increase the strength of the mortar
    D. improve the bearing capacity of the wall

18. Assume that excavation is taking place adjacent to a building on a spread footing and a   18._____
    building on pile foundations.
    Extreme care must be exercised in excavating

    A. near the pile-supported building because the soil in the area is of poor quality
    B. near a building on spread footings because the concrete footings may crack
    C. for a pile-supported foundation because heavy loads are involved
    D. near a building on spread footings because of the danger of undermining the foun-
       dations

19. An inspector inspecting a large building under construction inspected brickwork at 9 M.,   19._____
    formwork at 10 A.M., and concrete at 11 A.M. and did his office work in the afternoon. He
    followed the same pattern daily for months.
    This procedure is

    A. *bad* because not enough time is devoted to concrete work
    B. *bad* because the tradesmen know when the inspections will occur
    C. *good* because it is methodical and he does not miss any of the trades
    D. *good* because it gives equal amount of time to the important trades

20. If a supervisor finds a discrepancy between the plans and specifications, he should   20._____

    A. always follow the plans
    B. ask for an interpretation
    C. always follow the specifications
    D. follow the plans if the difference is in dimensions

———

KEY (CORRECT ANSWERS)

1.	B	11.	B
2.	D	12.	C
3.	B	13.	C
4.	A	14.	C
5.	A	15.	A
6.	D	16.	C
7.	C	17.	B
8.	B	18.	D
9.	A	19.	B
10.	A	20.	B

EXAMINATION SECTION
TEST 1

DIRECTIONS: Each question or incomplete statement is followed by several suggested answers or completions. Select the one that BEST answers the question or completes the statement. *PRINT THE LETTER OF THE CORRECT ANSWER IN THE SPACE AT THE RIGHT.*

1. A significant difference between ordinary contract law and construction contract law is that under most construction contracts,   1.____

    A. *breach of contract* is interpreted more widely
    B. a prime contractor's bid proposal is normally considered to be irrevocable after the bid opening and during the acceptance period prescribed in the bidding documents
    C. a subcontractor's bid is normally considered to be irrevocable even if the acceptance period is extended without his knowledge or consent
    D. an owner is not bound by oral agreements regarding the materials or workmanship of a project

2. Most negotiated construction contracts are on a _____ basis.   2.____

    A. cost-plus-fee   B. lump-sum
    C. unit-price   D. fee simple

3. When a specifier states outright the actual make, model, and catalog number of a product or the installation instructions of a manufacturer, he has written a _____ specification into the contract.   3.____

    A. reference   B. descriptive
    C. proprietary   D. performance

4. The written documents in a construction contract that describe the work to be done — including materials, equipment, construction systems, standards, and workmanship — requirements are commonly referred to as   4.____

    A. reference documents   B. drawings
    C. general conditions   D. specifications

5. According to the CSI Masterformat for specifications, each of the following would be listed in the General Requirements division of the specifications EXCEPT   5.____

    A. alternates   B. bonds and certificates
    C. maintenance   D. summary of work

6. In construction contract documents, invitations to bid are typically bound in the   6.____

    A. agreement   B. general conditions
    C. specifications   D. addenda

7. When substantial completion of a project has been achieved, it is customary for an inspection to be held to determine items that require completion or correction. The record of these items is known as a(n)   7.____

    A. supplementary condition   B. punch list
    C. escalator clause   D. change order

8. The manner in which construction contracts are most commonly terminated is by   8.____

    A. full and satisfactory performance by both parties
    B. proving impossibility of performance
    C. breach of contract by either party
    D. mutual agreement of both parties

9. On a unit-price project, a bid in which each bid item includes its own direct project cost plus its pro rata share of the project overhead, markup, bond, and tax is referred to as   9.____

    A. balanced   B. bonded
    C. weighted   D. cost-plus-percentage

10. Extensions of time in construction contracts are typically formalized by an instrument known as a(n)   10.____

    A. change order   B. squinter
    C. supplementary condition   D. easement

11. Under the terms of most cost-plus contracts, a common contract provision is for   11.____

    A. weekly or biweekly reimbursement of payrolls, and monthly reimbursement of all other costs, including a pro rata share of the contractor's fee
    B. monthly reimbursement of all costs including payroll and a pro rata share of the fee
    C. weekly reimbursement of all costs including payroll, and a monthly pro rata installment of the contractor's fee
    D. weekly or biweekly reimbursement of payrolls, and monthly reimbursement of all other costs except any portion of the contractor's fee, which is paid in full upon substantial completion

12. When open bidding is being used, it is necessary to include a prepared proposal form with the contract documents, because it   12.____

    A. helps in itemizing unbalanced bids
    B. exposes the different unit prices used by competing bidders
    C. is required by law
    D. ensures that all bids will be prepared and evaluated on the same basis

13. Where several different kinds or classes of similar materials are used, they should be described in a manner that permits some materials to be specified for every part of the building. This technique is a system known as the   13.____

    A. residuary legatee   B. subdivision
    C. criterion reference   D. variable proviso

14. A physical aspect of a construction site that differs materially from that indicated by the contract documents, or that is of an unusual nature and differs materially from the environment normally encountered, is described in the contract as a(n)   14.____

    A. supplementary condition   B. bid point
    C. changed condition   D. estoppel

15. Which of the following is a performance specification?   15.____

    A. Ceilings will be 2' x 2' lay-in acoustical panels.
    B. The heating system shall use #6 oil and shall be a hot water system.

C. Doors and other interior woodwork will have a natural finish.

D. Contractors shall install four inch ceramic tile throughout bathroom floor area.

16. Which of the following are generally TRUE of construction contract documents?   16.____
    I. Specific provisions prevail over general provisions.
    II. The handwritten version prevails over the typewritten version.
    III. In the event that inconsistencies exist where numbers are expressed in words and figures, the numbers govern.
    IV. If a conflict exists between drawings and specifications, the drawings usually take precedence.

The CORRECT answer is:

A. I, II   B. III, IV
C. I, II, IV   D. II, III, IV

17. For very large construction projects, an insurance program is sometimes used which combines all the interests involved in a construction project for insurance purposes with one insurer chosen by either the owner or the contractor. This type of arrangement is known as   17.____

A. comprehensive general liability insurance
B. umbrella excess liability coverage
C. wrap-up insurance policy
D. subrogation

18. In a cost-incentive contract, the most common share of savings awarded to a contractor is _____ percent.   18.____

A. 40   B. 50   C. 60   D. 75

19. In the CSI Masterformat for specifications, which of the following items would be described and listed in Division 9?   19.____

A. Carpet   B. Insulation
C. Rough carpentry   D. Pest control

20. The submission of a complimentary bid by a contractor is generally thought to be an acceptable practice when it is done for any of the following reasons EXCEPT to   20.____

A. fix prices and make the bidding process less competitive
B. keep the goodwill of the owner or engineer who solicits the bid
C. please an owner-client
D. obtain the refund of plan deposits

21. Which of the following specifications is most effectively written?   21.____

A. Each joint must be filled solid with mortar.
B. Each joint is to be filled solid with mortar.
C. Each joint shall be filled solid with mortar.
D. Fill each joint solid with mortar.

22. Which of the following is a duty of an architect-engineer under the terms of a typical construction contract?

    A. Authorizing a contractor's periodic payments
    B. Ensuring that workmanship and materials fulfill the requirements of drawings and specifications
    C. Issuing direct instructions as to the method or procedures used in construction operations
    D. Conducting property surveys that describe the project site

22.____

23. In a technical section of a construction contract, tests for soil compaction would be described in a subparagraph under the heading of

    A. materials/equipment   B. fabrication
    C. field quality control   D. project/site conditions

23.____

24. Which of the following is a form that authorizes a contractor to proceed with work until a formal change order can be processed?

    A. Writ of mandamus   B. Field order
    C. Presentment   D. Letter of intent

24.____

25. When included in a construction contract, completed operations insurance is a liability contract that covers which of the following damages?

    I. Injuries to persons
    II. Damage to property attributed to the operation
    III. Damage to the completed work itself
The CORRECT answer is:

    A. I only   B. III only   C. I, II   D. II, III

25.____

KEY (CORRECT ANSWERS)

1.	B	11.	A
2.	A	12.	D
3.	C	13.	A
4.	D	14.	C
5.	B	15.	B
6.	C	16.	A
7.	B	17.	C
8.	A	18.	B
9.	A	19.	A
10.	A	20.	A

21.	D
22.	B
23.	C
24.	B
25.	C

TEST 2

Each question or incomplete statement is followed by several suggested answers or completions. Select the one that BEST answers the question or completes the statement. *PRINT THE LETTER OF THE CORRECT ANSWER IN THE SPACE AT THE RIGHT.*

1. Design decisions and special project requirements recorded at the end of the design-development phase of document preparation are included in the   1.____

   A. addendum
   C. outline specification

   B. project manual
   D. supplementary conditions

2. The greatest apparent drawback to using product approval standards in the bidding of a construction project is that   2.____

   A. competition is limited
   B. the bidding period is extended
   C. bidders assume a greater risk in accepting products other than those specified
   D. relatively less flexibility

3. The general clauses of a construction contract are composed of each of the following EXCEPT   3.____

   A. specifications
   C. provisions of the agreement

   B. supplementary conditions
   D. general conditions

4. In specifications writing, the most common form of duplication is the use of a heading titled   4.____

   A. Work of Other Sections
   C. Work Not Included

   B. Scope of Work
   D. Duplication-Repetition

5. A common provision of construction contracts is that final payment is due the contractor   5.____

   A. 30 days after substantial completion
   B. at the end of the warranty period
   C. at the stated end of the contract period
   D. upon final completion

6. The MAIN advantage of the bidder's choice specification over the base bid specification is that   6.____

   A. product selection rests entirely with the architect or engineer
   B. greater competition is invited
   C. bid shopping is eliminated
   D. specifications are generally shorter

7. Sometimes, an owner will require that a contractor include in his bid a listing of the sub-contractors whose bids were used in the preparation of the prime contractor's proposal. The subcontractor listing requirement is primarily used by the owner for the purpose of   7.____

   A. estimating unit prices
   B. keeping the subcontractors subject to the owners' approval
   C. determining the percentage for a cost-plus-percentage contract
   D. discouraging bid shopping by the prime contractor

8. Special warranties that are written into construction contracts typically extend a term to   8.____

    A. 1 to 5 years   B. 5 to 10 years
    C. 2 to 20 years   D. 2 to lifetime

9. Of the following, which most clearly is considered a general release in full by a contractor   9.____
of all claims against the owner arising out of or in consequence of the work?

    A. Agreement to terminate the contract
    B. Submission to binding arbitration
    C. Acceptance of final payment
    D. Completion of the work specified in the contract

10. A project manual is typically recorded toward the final review of the _____ phase of doc-   10.____
ument preparation.

    A. construction documents   B. schematic design
    C. design-development   D. evaluation

11. Which of the following Division headings appears EARLIEST in the CSI Masterformat of   11.____
specifications?

    A. Wood and plastics
    B. Thermal and moisture protection
    C. Sitework
    D. Concrete

12. In a typical technical section, the criteria by which the subcontractor determines that the   12.____
substrates to receive his work are sound, proper, and free of defects are included in the
subparagraphs under the heading of

    A. examination   B. preparation
    C. field quality control   D. mixes

13. For a contractor, each of the following is a potential disadvantage associated with grant-   13.____
ing an extension for the owner's acceptance period EXCEPT

    A. the potential for rises in labor wages
    B. the forfeiture of bid bonds
    C. the delaying of material orders by price advances
    D. a subcontractor or supplier's unwillingness to stand by earlier price quotes

14. What is the term for bidding requirements, contract forms, contract conditions, and spec-   14.____
ifications all bound collectively?

    A. Project manual   B. Conditions
    C. Contract forms   D. Master documents

15. Which of the following descriptions would NOT appear in Part 1 of a technical section   15.____
that follows the CSI standard format?

    A. Submittals   B. Equipment
    C. Delivery, storage, and handling   D. Schedules

16. Which of the following is a disadvantage associated with the cost-plus-percentage con- 16.____
    tract?

    A. There are no direct incentives for the contractor to minimize construction costs.
    B. It is not suitable for work whose scope and nature are poorly defined at the outset
       of operations.
    C. It is considered unsuitable for public projects.
    D. It does not offer much flexibility in handling emergency situations.

17. In construction contracts, the term of the general warranty typically does not exceed 17.____

    A. 90 days   B. 6 months   C. 1 year   D. 2 years

18. In a construction contract, what is the term for a word description of a basic trade or 18.____
    material installation which outlines the quality of material to be used and the quality of
    workmanship to be practiced in its installation?

    A. Annotated drawing   B. Technical section
    C. Standard reference   D. Specification division

19. When an addendum is added to a construction contract, which of the following elements 19.____
    is typically included FIRST?

    A. Date of addendum
    B. Opening remarks and instructions
    C. Addendum and addendum number
    D. Name of architect/engineer or issuing agency

20. The main DISADVANTAGE associated with the use of alternates in the bidding process 20.____
    is that they

    A. decrease the security of individual bids
    B. complicate the bidding process and may increase inaccuracies
    C. are only effective when they are subtractive, rather than additive
    D. do not give the owner a clear idea of how to minimize costs

21. In a technical section written to conform to the CSI standard format, Part 2 would include 21.____
    descriptions of

    A. preparation   B. references
    C. field quality control   D. materials

22. In a typical project manual, which of the following elements appears FIRST? 22.____

    A. Bid bond   B. Schedule of drawings
    C. Agreement   D. General conditions

23. The insurance considerations of a construction contract, especially those governing lia- 23.____
    bility, are typically incorporated into the

    A. agreement   B. general conditions
    C. specifications   D. addenda

24. Written or graphic instruments issued after the execution of a contract, which alter con-   24.____
tract documents by additions, deletions, or corrections, are known specifically as

   A. contract modifications   B. change orders
   C. addenda   D. supplementary conditions

25. When a progress payments are part of a construction contract, it is common for a con-   25.____
tractor to apply for a payment
     I. when a prescribed amount of quantified construction costs have been
        expended
    II. on completion of designated phases of the work
   III. a prescribed number of days before it is due under the payment schedule
        written into the contract
The CORRECT answer is:

   A. II *only*   B. I or III
   C. II or III   D. I, II, or III

KEY (CORRECT ANSWERS)

1.	C		11.	C
2.	B		12.	A
3.	A		13.	B
4.	B		14.	A
5.	A		15.	D
6.	B		16.	A
7.	D		17.	C
8.	C		18.	B
9.	C		19.	D
10.	A		20.	B

21.	D
22.	C
23.	B
24.	A
25.	C

DOCUMENTS AND FORMS
PREPARING WRITTEN MATERIALS

EXAMINATION SECTION
TEST 1

DIRECTIONS : Each question or incomplete statement is followed by several suggested answers or completions. Select the one that BEST answers the question or completes the statement. *PRINT THE LETTER OF THE CORRECT ANSWER IN THE SPACE AT THE RIGHT.*

1. Of the following types of documents, it is MOST important to retain and file   1._____

    A. working drafts of reports that have been submitted in final form
    B. copies of letters of good will which conveyed a message that could not be handled by phone
    C. interoffice orders for materials which have been received and verified
    D. interoffice memoranda regarding the routine of standard forms

2. The MAXIMUM number of 2 3/4" x 4 1/4" size forms which may be obtained from one ream of 17" x 22" paper is   2._____

    A. 4,000   B. 8,000   C. 12,000   D. 16,000

3. On a general organization chart, staff positions NORMALLY should be pictured   3._____

    A. directly above the line positions to which they report
    B. to the sides of the main flow lines
    C. within the box of the highest level subordinate positions pictured
    D. directly below the line positions which report to them

4. When an administrator is diagramming an office layout, of the following, his PRIMARY job *generally* should be to indicate the   4._____

    A. lighting intensities that will be required by each operator
    B. noise level that will be produced by the various equip ment employed in the office
    C. direction of the work flow and the distance involved in each transfer
    D. durability of major pieces of office equipment currently in use or to be utilized

5. One common guideline or rule-of-thumb ratio for evaluating the efficiency of files is the number of records requested divided by the number of records filed. *Generally,* if this ratio is very low, it would point MOST directly to the need for   5._____

    A. improving the indexing and coding systems
    B. improving the charge-out procedures
    C. exploring the need for transferring records from active storage to the archives
    D. exploring the need to encourage employees to keep more records in their private files

6. The GREATEST percentage of money spent on preparing and keeping the usual records in an office *generally* is expended for which one of the following?

    A. Renting space in which to place the record-keeping equipment
    B. Paying salaries of record-preparing and record-keeping personnel
    C. Depreciation of purchased record-preparation and record-keeping machines
    D. Paper and forms upon which to place the records

6.____

7. In a certain office, file folders are constantly being removed from the files for use by administrators. At the same time, new material is coming in to be filed in some of these folders.
Of the following, the BEST way to avoid delays in filing of the new material and to keep track of the removed folders is to

    A. keep a sheet listing all folders removed from the file, who has them, and a follow-update to check on their return; attach to this list new material received for filing
    B. put an "out" slip in the place of any file folder removed, telling what folder is missing, date removed, and who has it; file new material received at front of files
    C. put a temporary "out" folder in place of the one removed, giving title or subject, date removed, and who has it; put into this temporary folder any new material received
    D. keep a list of all folders removed and who has them; forward any new material received for filing while a folder is out to the person who has it

7.____

8. Folders labeled "Miscellaneous" should be used in an alphabetic filing system MAINLY to

    A. provide quick access to recent material
    B. avoid setting up individual folders for infrequent correspondence
    C. provide temporary storage for less important documents
    D. temporarily hold papers which will not fit into already crowded individual folders

8.____

9. Out-of-date and seldom-used records should be removed periodically from the files because

    A. overall responsibility for records will be transferred to the person in charge of the central storage files
    B. duplicate copies of every record are not needed
    C. valuable filing space will be regained and the time needed to find a current record will be cut down
    D. worthwhile suggestions on improving the filing system will result whenever this is done

9.____

10. Of the following, the BEST reason for discarding certain material from office files would be that the

    A. files are crowded
    B. material in the files is old
    C. material duplicates information obtainable from other sources in the files
    D. material is referred to most often by employees in an adjoining office

10.____

11. Of the following, the MAIN factor contributing to the expense of maintaining an office pro-   11.____
cedure manual would be the

    A. infrequent use of the manual
    B. need to revise it regularly
    C. cost of loose-leaf binders
    D. high cost of printing

12. The suggestion that memos or directives which circulate among subordinates be initialed   12.____
by each employee is a

    A. *poor one,* because, with modern copying machines, it would be possible to supply
every subordinate with a copy of each message for his personal use
    B. *good one,* because it relieves the supervisor of blame for the action of subordi-
nates who have read and initialed the messages
    C. *poor one,* because initialing the memo or directive is no guarantee that the subordi-
nate has read the material
    D. *good one,* because it can be used as a record by the supervisor to show that his
subordinates have received the message and were responsible for reading it

13. Of the following, the MOST important reason for micro filming office records is to   13.____

    A. save storage space needed to keep records
    B. make it easier to get records when needed
    C. speed up the classification of information
    D. shorten the time which records must be kept

14. Your office filing cabinets have become so overcrowded that it is difficult to use the files.   14.____
Of the following, the *most* desirable step for you to take FIRST to relieve this situation
would be to

    A. assign your assistant to spend some time each day re-viewing the material in the
files and to give you his recommendations as to what material may be discarded
    B. discard all material which has been in the files more than a given number of years
    C. submit a request for additional filing cabinets in your next budget request
    D. transfer enough material to the central storage room of your agency to give you the
amount of additional filing space needed

15. In indexing names of business firms and other organizations, one of the rules to be fol-   15.____
lowed is:

    A. The word "and" is considered an indexing unit.
    B. When a firm name includes the full name of a person who is not well known, the
person's first name is considered as the first indexing unit.
    C. Usually, the units in a firm name are indexed in the order in which they are written.
    D. When a firm's name is made up of single letters (such as ABC Corp.), the letters
taken together are considered as more than one indexing unit.

16. Assume that your unit processes confidential forms which are submitted by persons   16.____
seeking financial assistance. An individual comes to your office, gives you his name, and
states that he would like to look over a form which he sent in about a week ago because
he believes he omitted some important information.
Of the following, the BEST thing for you to do *first* is to

A. locate the proper form
B. call the individual's home telephone number to verify his identity
C. ask the individual if he has proof of his identity
D. call the security office

17. An employee has been assigned to open her division head's mail and place it on his   17.____
desk. One day, the employee opens a letter which she then notices is marked "Personal."
Of the following, the BEST action for her to take is to

A. write "Personal" on the letter and staple the envelope to the back of the letter
B. ignore the matter and treat the letter the same way as the others
C. give it to another division head to hold until her own division head comes into the
office
D. leave the letter in the envelope and write "Sorry-opened by mistake" on the enve-
lope, and initial it

18. The MOST important reason for having a filing system is to   18.____

A. get papers out of the way
B. have a record of everything that has happened
C. retain information to justify your actions
D. enable rapid retrieval of information

19. The system of filing which is used MOST frequently is called   19.____

A. alphabetic filing
C. geographic filing
B. alphanumeric filing
D. numeric filing

20. In judging the adequacy of a standard office form, which of the following is LEAST impor-   20.____
tant?

A. Date of the form
C. Size of the form
B. Legibility of the form
D. Design of the form

21. Assume that, the letters and reports which are dictated to you fall into a few distinct sub-   21.____
ject-matter areas.
The practice of trying to familiarize yourself with the terminology in these areas is

A. *good,* because you will have a basis for commenting on the dictated material
B. *good,* because it will be easier to take the dictation at the rate at which it is given
C. *poor,* because the functions and policies of an office are not of your concern
D. *poor,* because it will take too much time away from your assigned work

22. A letter was dictated on June 9 and was ready to be typed on June 12. The letter   22.____
was typed on June 13, signed on June 14, and mailed on June 14. The date that,
ordinarily, should have appeared on the letter is

A. June 9
C. June 13
B. June 12
D. June 14

23. Of the following, the BEST reason for putting the *"key point"* at the beginning of a letter is that it   23.____

    A. may save time for the reader
    B. is standard practice in writing letters
    C. will more likely be typed correctly
    D. cannot logically be placed elsewhere

24. As a supervisor, you have been asked to attend committee meetings and take the minutes.   24.____
The body of such minutes, *generally,* consists of

    A. the date and place of the meeting and the list of persons present
    B. an exact verbatim report of everything that was said by each person who spoke
    C. a clear description of each matter discussed and the action decided on
    D. the agenda of the meeting

25. When typing a rough draft from a transcribing machine, a stenographer under your supervision reaches a spot on the tape that is virtually inaudible.   25.____
Of the following, the MOST advisable action that you should recommend to her is to

    A. guess what the dictator intended to say based on what he said in the parts that are clear
    B. ask the dictator to listen to his unsatisfactory dictation
    C. leave an appropriate amount of space for that portion that is inaudible
    D. stop typing the draft and send a note to the dictator identifying the item that could not be completed

---

KEYS (CORRECT ANSWERS)

1.	D	11.	B
2.	D	12.	D
3.	B	13.	A
4.	C	14.	A
5.	C	15.	C
6.	B	16.	C
7.	C	17.	D
8.	B	18.	D
9.	C	19.	A
10.	C	20.	A

21.	B
22.	D
23.	A
24.	C
25.	C

TEST 2

DIRECTIONS : Each question or incomplete statement is followed by several suggested answers or completions. Select the one that BEST answers the question or completes the statement. *PRINT THE LETTER OF THE CORRECT ANSWER IN THE SPACE AT THE RIGHT.*

1. To tell a newly employed clerk to fill a top drawer of a four-drawer cabinet with heavy folders which will be often used and to keep lower drawers only partly filled, is   1.____

   A. *good,* because a tall person would have to bend unnecessarily if he had to use a lower drawer
   B. *bad,* because the file cabinet may tip over when the top drawer is opened
   C. *good,* because it is the most easily reachable drawer for the average person
   D. *bad,* because a person bending down at another drawer may accidentally bang his head on the bottom of the drawer when he straightens up

2. If you have requisitioned a "ream" of paper in order to duplicate a single page office announcement, how many announcements can be printed from the one package of paper?   2.____

   A. 200   B. 500   C. 700   D. 1,000

3. In the operations of a government agency, a voucher is ORDINARILY used to   3.____

   A. refer someone to the agency for a position or assignment
   B. certify that an agency's records of financial transactions are accurate
   C. order payment from agency funds of a stated amount to an individual
   D. enter a statement of official opinion in the records of the agency

4. Of the following types of cards used in filing systems, the one which is generally MOST helpful in locating records which might be filed under more than one subject is the   4.____

   A. out card   B. tickler card
   C. cross-reference card   D. visible index card

5. The type of filing system in which one does NOT need to refer to a card index in order to find the folder is called   5.____

   A. alphabetic   B. geographic
   C. subject   D. locational

6. Of the following, records management is LEAST concerned with   6.____

   A. the development of the best method for retrieving important information
   B. deciding what records should be kept
   C. deciding the number of appointments a client will need
   D. determining the types of folders to be used

7. If records are continually removed from a set of files without "charging" them to the borrower, the filing system will soon become ineffective.   7.____
   Of the following terms, the one which is NOT applied to a form used in the charge-out system is a

   A. requisition card   B. out-folder
   C. record retrieval form   D. substitution card

8. A new clerk has been told to put 500 cards in alphabetical order. Another clerk suggests that she divide the cards into four groups such as A to F, G to L, M to R, and S to Z, and then alphabetize these four smaller groups. The suggested method is

    A. *poor*, because the clerk will have to handle the sheets more than once and will waste time
    B. *good* because it saves time, is more accurate, and is less tiring
    C. *good,* because she will not have to concentrate on it so much when it is in smaller groups
    D. *poor,* because this method is much more tiring than straight alphabetizing

8._____

9. In Microsoft Excel, data and records are entered into

    A. pages   B. forms   C. cells   D. contracts

9._____

10. Suppose a clerk has been given pads of pre-printed forms to use when taking phone messages for others in her office. The clerk is then observed using scraps of paper and not the forms for writing her messages.
It should be explained that the BEST reason for using the forms is that

    A. they act as a check list to make sure that the important information is taken
    B. she is expected to do her work in the same way as others in the office
    C. they make sure that unassigned paper is not wasted on phone messages
    D. learning to use these forms will help train her to use more difficult forms

10._____

11. The high-speed printing process used for producing large quantities of SUPERIOR quality copy and cost efficency is called

    A. photocopying   B. laser printing
    C. inkjet printing   D. word processing

11._____

12. Of the following, the MAIN reason a stock clerk keeps a perpetual inventory of supplies in the storeroom is that such an inventory will

    A. eliminate the need for a physical inventory
    B. provide a continuous record of supplies on hand
    C. indicate whether a shipment of supplies is satisfactory
    D. dictate the terms of the purchase order

12._____

13. As a supervisor, you may be required to handle different types of correspondence. Of the following types of letters, it would be MOST important to promptly seal which kind of letter?

    A. One marked "confidential"
    B. Those containing enclosures
    C. Any letter to be sent airmail
    D. Those in which copies will be sent along with the original

13._____

14. While opening incoming mail, you notice that one letter indicates that an enclosure was to be included but, even after careful inspection, you are not able to find the information to which this refers.
Of the following, the thing that you should do FIRST is

    A. replace the letter in its envelope and return it to the sender
    B. file the letter until the sender's office mails the missing information

14._____

    C.   type out a letter to the sender informing him of his error
    D.   make a notation in the margin of the letter that the enclosure was omitted

15.   You have been given a check list and assigned the responsibility of inspecting certain   15.____
       equipment in the various offices of your agency.
       Which of the following is the GREATEST advantage of the check list?

    A.   It indicates which equipment is in greatest demand.
    B.   Each piece of equipment on the check list will be checked only once.
    C.   It helps to insure that the equipment listed will not be overlooked.
    D.   The equipment listed suggests other equipment you should look for.

16.   The BEST way to evaluate the overall state of completion of a construction project is to   16.____
       check the progress estimate against the

    A.   inspection work sheet
    B.   construction schedule
    C.   inspector's check list
    D.   equipment maintenance schedule

17.   The usual contract for agency work includes a section entitled, "Instructions to Bidders,"   17.____
       which states that the

    A.   contractor agrees that he has made his own examination and will make no claim
         for damages on account of errors or omissions
    B.   contractor shall not make claims for damages of any discrepancy, error or omission
         in any plans
    C.   estimates of quantities and calculations are guaranteed by the agency to be cor-
         rect and are deemed to be a representation of the conditions affecting the work
    D.   plans, measurements, dimensions and conditions under which the work is to be
         performed are guaranteed by the agency

18.   In order to avoid disputes over payments for extra work in a contract for construction, the   18.____
       BEST procedure to follow would be to

    A.   have contractor submit work progress reports daily
    B.   insert a special clause in the contract specifications
    C.   have a representative on the job at all times to verify conditions
    D.   allocate a certain percentage of the cost of the job to cover such expenses

19.   Prior to the installation of equipment called for in the specifications, the contractor is   19.____
       USUALLY required to submit for approval

    A.   sets of shop drawings
    B.   a set of revised specifications
    C.   a detailed description of the methods of work to be used
    D.   a complete list of skilled and unskilled tradesmen he proposes to use

20. During the actual construction work, the CHIEF value of a construction schedule is to   20.____
    A. insure that the work will be done on time
    B. reveal whether production is falling behind
    C. show how much equipment and material is required for the project
    D. furnish data as to the methods and techniques of construction operations

_____

KEYS (CORRECT ANSWERS)

1.	B		11.	B
2.	B		12.	B
3.	C		13.	A
4.	C		14.	D
5.	A		15.	C
6.	C		16.	B
7.	C		17.	A
8.	B		18.	C
9.	C		19.	A
10.	A		20.	B

_____

REPORT WRITING
EXAMINATION SECTION
TEST 1

DIRECTIONS: Each question or incomplete statement is followed by several suggested answers or completions. Select the one that BEST answers the question or completes the statement. *PRINT THE LETTER OF THE CORRECT ANSWER IN THE SPACE AT THE RIGHT.*

Questions 1-3.

DIRECTIONS: Questions 1 to 3 are based on the following example of a report. The report consists of ten numbered sentences, some of which are *not* consistent with the principles of good report writing.

(1) On the evening of February 24, Roscoe and Leroy, two members of the "Red Devils," were entering with a bottle of wine in their hands. (2) It was unusually good wine for these boys to buy, (3) I told them to give me the bottle and they refused, and added that they wouldn"t let anyone "put them out." (4) I told them they were entitled to have a good time, but they could not do it the way they wanted; there were certain rules they had to observe, (5) At this point, Roscoe said he had seen me box at camp and suggested that Leroy not accept my offer. (6) Then I said firmly that the admission fee did not give them the authority to tell me what to do. (7) I also told them that, if they thought I would fight them over such a matter, they were sadly mistaken. (8) I added, however, that we could go to the gym right now and settle it another way if they wished. (9) Leroy immediately said that he was sorry, he had not understood the rules, and he did not want his quarter back. (10) On the other hand, they would not give up their bottle either, so they left the premises..

1. Only material that is relevant to the main thought of a report should be included. Which of the following sentences from the report contains material which is LEAST relevant to this report? Sentence   1.____

   A. 2   B. 3   C. 8   D. 9

2. A good report should be arranged in logical order. Which of the following sentences from the report does NOT appear in its proper sequence in the report? Sentence   2.____

   A. 3   B. 5   C. 7   D. 9

3. Reports should include all essential information.   3.____
   Of the following, the MOST important fact that is *missing* from this report is:

   A. Who was involved in the incident
   B. How the incident was resolved
   C. When the incident took place
   D. Where the incident took place

4. The MOST serious of the following faults *commonly* found in explanatory reports is 4.____

   A. the use of slang terms   B. excessive details
   C. C. personal bias   D. redundancy

5. In reviewing a report he has prepared to submit to his superiors, a supervisor finds that 5.____
   his paragraphs are a typewritten page long and decides to make some revisions.
   Of the following, the MOST important question he should ask about each paragraph
   is:

   A. Are the words too lengthy?
   B. Is the idea under discussion too abstract?
   C. Is more than one central thought being expressed?
   D. Are the sentences too long?

6. The summary or findings of a long management report intended for the typical manager 6.____
   should, *generally,* appear

   A. at the very beginning of the report
   B. at the end of the report
   C. throughout the report
   D. in the middle of the report

7. In preparing a report that includes several tables, if not otherwise instructed, the typist 7.____
   should *most properly* include a list of tables

   A. in the introductory part of the report
   B. at the end of each chapter in the body of the report
   C. in the supplementary part of the report as an appendix
   D. in the supplementary part of the report as a part of the index

8. When typing a preliminary draft of a report, the one of the following which you should 8.____
   generally NOT do is to

   A. erase typing errors and deletions rather than "X"ing them out
   B. leave plenty of room at the top, bottom and sides of each page
   C. make only the number of copies that you are asked to make
   D. type double or triple space

9. When you determine the methods of emphasis you will use in typing the titles, headings 9.____
   and subheadings of a report, the one of the following which it is MOST important to keep
   in mind is that

   A. all headings of the same rank should be typed in the same way
   B. all headings should be typed in the single style which is most pleasing to the eye
   C. headings should not take up more than one third of the page width
   D. only one method should be used for all headings, whatever their rank

10. The one of the following ways in which inter-office memoranda *differ* from long formal 10.____
    reports is that they, *generally,*

    A. are written as if the reader is familiar with the vocabulary and technical background
       of the writer
    B. do not have a "subject line" which describes the major topic covered in the text

C. include a listing of reference materials which support the memo writer's conclusions
D. require that a letter of transmittal be attached

11. It is *preferable* to print information on a field report rather than write it out longhand MAINLY because

11.____

A. printing takes less time to write than writing longhand
B. printing is usually easier to read than longhand writing
C. longhand writing on field reports is not acceptable in court cases
D. printing occupies less space on a report than longhand writing

12. Of the following characteristics of a written report, the one that is MOST important is its

12.____

A. length   B. accuracy   C. organization   D. grammar

13. A written report to your superior contains many spelling errors.
Of the following statements relating to spelling errors, the one that is *most nearly* correct is that

13.____

A. this is unimportant as long as the meaning of the report is clear
B. readers of the report will ignore the many spelling errors
C. readers of the report will get a poor opinion of the writer of the report
D. spelling errors are unimportant as long as the grammar is correct

14. Written reports to your superior should have the same general arrangement and layout. The BEST reason for this requirement is that the

14.____

A. report will be more accurate
B. report will be more complete
C. person who reads the report will know what the subject of the report is
D. person who reads the report will know where to look for information in the report

15. The first paragraph of a report usually contains detailed information on the subject of the report.
Of the following, the BEST reason for this requirement is to enable the

15.____

A. reader to quickly find the subject of the report
B. typist to immediately determine the subject of the report so that she will understand what she is typing
C. clerk to determine to whom copies of the report shall be routed
D. typist to quickly determine how many copies of the report will be needed

16. Of the following statements concerning reports, the one which is LEAST valid is:

16.____

A. A case report should contain factual material to support conclusions made.
B. An extremely detailed report may be of less value than a brief report giving the essential facts.
C. Highly technical language should be avoided as far as possible in preparing a report to be used at a court trial.
D. The position of the important facts in a report does not influence the emphasis placed on them by the reader.

17. Suppose that you realize that you have made an error in a report that has been for-   17.____
    warded to another unit. You know that this error is not likely to be discovered for some
    time.
    Of the following, the MOST advisable course of action for you to take is to

    A. approach the supervisor of the other unit on an informal basis, and ask him to cor-
       rect the error
    B. say nothing about it since most likely one error will not invalidate the entire report
    C. tell your supervisor immediately that you have made an error so that it may be cor-
       rected, if necessary
    D. wait until the error is discovered and then admit that you had made it

18. In a report, words in a sentence must be arranged properly to make sure that the   18.____
    intended meaning of the sentence is clear.
    The sentence below that does NOT make sense because a clause has been sepa-
    rated from the word on which its meaning depends is:

    A. To be a good writer, clarity is necessary.
    B. To be a good writer, you must write clearly.
    C. You must write clearly to be a good writer.
    D. Clarity is necessary to good writing.

19. The use of a graph to show statistical data in a report is *superior* to a table because it 19.____

    A. emphasizes approximations
    B. emphasizes facts and relationships more dramatically
    C. presents data more accurately
    D. is easily understood by the average reader

20. Of the following, the degree of formality required of a written report is, *most likely* to 20.____
    depend on the

    A. subject matter of the report
    B. frequency of its occurrence
    C. amount of time available for its preparation
    D. audience for whom the report is intended

Questions 21-25.

DIRECTIONS: Questions 21 through 25 consist of sets of four sentences lettered A, B, C, and
               For each question, choose the sentence which is grammatically and stylisti-
               cally *most appropriate* for use in a *formal* WRITTEN REPORT.

21.   A. It is recommended, therefore, that the impasse panelhearings are to be convened   21.____
         on September 30.
      B. It is therefore recommended that the impasse panel hearings be convened on
         September 30.
      C. Therefore, it is recommended to convene the impasse panel hearings on Sep-
         tember 30.
      D. It is recommended that the impasse panel hearings therefore should be con-
         vened on September 30.

22.   A. Penalties have been assessed for violating the TaylorLaw by several unions.   22.____
      B. When they violated provisions of the Taylor Law, several unions were later penalized.
      C. Several unions have been penalized for violating provisions of the Taylor Law.
      D. Several unions' violating provisions of the Taylor Law resulted in them being penalized.

23.   A. The number of disputes settled through mediation has increased significantly over   23.____
         the past two years.
      B. The number of disputes settled through mediation are increasing significantly over two-year periods.
      C. Over the past two years, through mediation, the number of disputes settled increased significantly.
      D. There is a significant increase over the past two years of the number of disputes settled through mediation.

24.   A. The union members will vote to determine if the contract is to be approved.   24.____
      B. It is not yet known whether the union members will ratify the proposed contract.
      C. When the union members vote, that will determine the new contract.
      D. Whether the union members will ratify the proposed contract, it is not yet known.

25.   A. The parties agreed to an increase in fringe benefits in return for greater work productivity.   25.____
      B. Greater productivity was agreed to be provided in return for increased fringe benefits.
      C. Productivity and fringe benefits are interrelated; the higher the former, the more the latter grows.
      D. The contract now provides that the amount of fringe benefits will depend upon the level of output by the workers.

KEY (CORRECT ANSWERS)

1.	A		11.	B
2.	B		12.	B
3.	D		13.	C
4.	C		14.	D
5.	C		15.	A
6.	A		16.	D
7.	A		17.	C
8.	A		18.	A
9.	A		19.	B
10.	A		20.	D

21.	B
22.	C
23.	A
24.	B
25.	A

TEST 2

DIRECTIONS: Answer Questions 1 through 4 on the basis of the following report which was prepared by a supervisor for inclusion in his agency's annual report.

Line
 #
1   On Oct. 13, I was assigned to study the salaries paid
2   to clerical employees in various titles by the city and by
3   private industry in the area.
4   In order to get the data I needed, I called Mr. Johnson at
5   the Bureau of the Budget and the payroll officers at X Corp. —
6   a brokerage house, Y Co. — an insurance company, and Z Inc. —
7   a publishing firm. None of them was available and I had to call
8   all of them again the next day.
9   When I finally got the information I needed, I drew up a
10   chart, which is attached. Note that not all of the companies I
11   contacted employed people at all the different levels used in the
12   city service.
13   The conclusions I draw from analyzing this information is
14   as follows: The city's entry-level salary is about average for
15   the region; middle-level salaries are generally higher in the
16   city government than in private industry; but salaries at the
17   highest levels in private industry are better than city em-
18   ployees' pay.

1.   Which of the following criticisms about the style in which this report is written is MOST   1._____
     valid?

     A.   It is too informal.   B.   It is too concise.
     C.   It is too choppy.   D.   The syntax is too complex.

2.   Judging from the statements made in the report, the method followed by this employee in   2._____
     performing his research was

     A.   *good;* he contacted a representative sample of businesses in the area
     B.   *poor;* he should have drawn more definite conclusions
     C.   *good;* he was persistent in collecting information
     D.   *poor;* he did not make a thorough study

3.   One sentence in this report contains a grammatical error. This sentence *begins* on line   3._____
     number

     A.   4   B.   7   C.   10   D.   13

4.   The type of information given in this report which should be presented in footnotes or in   4._____
     an appendix, is the

A. purpose of the study
B. specifics about the businesses contacted
C. reference to the chart
D. conclusions drawn by the author

5. Of the following, a DISTINGUISHING characteristic of a written report intended for the head of your agency as compared to a report prepared for a lower-echelon staff member is that the report for the agency head should, *usually,* include 5.____

    A. considerably more detail, especially statistical data
    B. the essential details in an abbreviated form
    C. all available source material
    D. an annotated bibliography

6. Assume that you are asked to write a lengthy report for use by the administrator of your agency, the subject of which is "The Impact of Proposed New Data Processing Operations on Line Personnel" in your agency. You decide that the *most appropriate* type of report for you to prepare is an analytical report, including recommendations.
The MAIN reason for your decision is that 6.____

    A. the subject of the report is extremely complex
    B. large sums of money are involved
    C. the report is being prepared for the administrator
    D. you intend to include charts and graphs

7. Assume that you are preparing a report based on a survey dealing with the attitudes of employees in Division X regarding proposed new changes in compensating employees for working overtime. Three percent of the respondents to the survey voluntarily offer an unfavorable opinion on the method of assigning overtime work, a question not speci-cally asked of the employees.
On the basis of this information, the MOST appropriate and significant of the following comments for you to make in the report with regard to employees' attitudes on assigning overtime work is that 7.____

    A. an insignificant percentage of employees dislike the method of assigning overtime work
    B. three percent of the employees in Division X dislike the method of assigning overtime work
    C. three percent of the sample selected for the survey voiced an unfavorable opinion on the method of assigning overtime work
    D. some employees voluntarily voiced negative feelings about the method of assigning overtime work, making it impossible to determine the extent of this attitude

8. Assume that you have been asked to prepare a narrative summary of the monthly reports submitted by employees in your division.
In preparing your summary of this month's reports, the FIRST step to take is to 8.____

    A. read through the reports, noting their general content and any unusual features
    B. decide how many typewritten pages your summary should contain
    C. make a written summary of each separate report, so that you will not have to go back to the original reports again
    D. ask each employee which points he would prefer to see emphasized in your summary

9. Assume that an administrative officer is writing a brief report to his superior outlining the advantages of matrix organization. Of the following, it would be INCORRECT to state that

    A. in matrix organization, a project is emphasized by designating one individual as the focal point for all matters pertaining to it
    B. utilization of manpower can be flexible in matrix organization because a reservoir of specialists is maintained in the line operations
    C. the usual line-staff management is generally reversed in matrix organization
    D. in matrix organization, responsiveness to project needs is generally faster due to establishing needed communication lines and decision points

9.____

10. Written reports dealing with inspections of work and installations SHOULD be

    A. as long and detailed as practicable
    B. phrased with personal interpretations
    C. limited to the important facts of the inspection
    D. technically phrased to create an impression on superiors

10.____

11. It is important to use definite, exact words in preparing a descriptive report and to avoid, as much as possible, nouns that have vague meanings and, possibly, a different meaning for the reader than for the author.
Which of the following sentences contains only nouns that are *definite* and *exact*?

    A. The free enterprise system should be vigorously encouraged in the United States.
    B. Arley Swopes climbed Mount Everest three times last year.
    C. Beauty is a characteristic of all the women at the party.
    D. Gil Noble asserts that he is a real democrat.

11.____

12. One way of shortening an unnecessarily long report is to reduce sentence length by eliminating the use of several words where a single one that does not alter the meaning will do.
Which of the following sentences CANNOT be shortened without losing some of its information content?

    A. After being polished, the steel ball bearings ran at maximum speed.
    B. After the close of the war, John Taylor was made the recipient of a pension.
    C. In this day and age, you can call anyone up on the telephone.
    D. She is attractive in appearance, but she is a rather selfish person.

12.____

13. Employees are required to submit written reports of all unusual occurrences promptly. The BEST reason for such promptness is that the

    A. report may be too long if made at one's convenience
    B. employee will not be so likely to forget to make the report
    C. report will tend to be more accurate as to facts
    D. employee is likely to make a better report under pressure

13.____

14. In making a report, it is poor practice to erase information on the report in order to make a change because

    A. there may be a question of what was changed and why it was changed
    B. you are likely to erase through the paper and tear the report

14.____

C. the report will no longer look neat and presentable
D. the duplicate copies will be smudged

15. The one of the following which BEST describes a periodic report is that it   15._____

   A. provides a record of accomplishments for a given time span and a comparison with similar time spans in the past
   B. covers the progress made in a project that has been postponed
   C. integrates, summarizes, and, perhaps, interprets published data on technical or scientific material
   D. describes a decision, advocates a policy or action, and presents facts in support of the writer's position

16. The PRIMARY purpose of including pictorial illustrations in a formal report is *usually* to   16._____

   A. amplify information which has been adequately treated verbally
   B. present details that are difficult to describe verbally
   C. provide the reader with a pleasant, momentary distraction
   D. present supplementary information incidental to the main ideas developed in the report

_____

KEY (CORRECT ANSWERS)

1.	A		6.	A
2.	D		7.	D
3.	D		8.	A
4.	B		9.	C
5.	B		10.	C

11.	B
12.	A
13.	C
14.	A
15.	A
16.	B

_____

ARITHMETICAL REASONING

EXAMINATION SECTION
TEST 1

DIRECTIONS: Each question or incomplete statement is followed by several suggested answers or completions. Select the one that BEST answers the question or completes the statement. *PRINT THE LETTER OF THE CORRECT ANSWER IN THE SPACE AT THE RIGHT.*

1. If it takes 2 men 9 days to do a job, how many men are needed to do the same job in 3 days?

    A. 4   B. 5   C. 6   D. 7

1.____

2. Suppose that a department operates 1,644 buildings. If one employee is needed for every 2 buildings, and one foreman is needed for every 18 employees, the number of foremen needed is CLOSEST to

    A. 45   B. 50   C. 55   D. 60

2.____

3. If 60 bars of soap cost the same as 2 gallons of wax, how many bars of soap can be bought for the price of 5 gallons of wax?

    A. 120   B. 150   C. 180   D. 300

3.____

4. An employee waxes 275 sq.ft. of floor on Monday, 352 sq.ft. on Tuesday, 179 sq.ft. on Wednesday, and 302 sq.ft. on Thursday.
In order to average 280 sq.ft. of floor waxed a day, how many square feet of floor must he wax on Friday?

    A. 264   B. 278   C. 292   D. 358

4.____

5. A project covers 35 acres altogether. Lawns, playgrounds, and walks take up 28 acres and the rest is given over to buildings.
What percentage of the total area is given over to buildings?

    A. 7%   B. 20%   C. 25%   D. 28%

5.____

6. When preparing for a mopping operation, fill the standard 16 quart bucket to the 3/4 full mark with warm water. Then add detergent at the rate of 2 oz. per gallon of water and disinfectant at the rate of 1 oz. to 3 gallons of water. According to these directions, the amount of detergent and disinfectant to add to 3/4 of a bucket of warm water is _____ oz. detergent and _____ oz. disinfectant.

    A. 4; 1/2   B. 5; 3/4   C. 6; 1   D. 8; 1 1/4

6.____

7. If corn brooms weigh 32 lbs. a dozen, the average weight of one corn broom is CLOSEST to _____ lbs. _____ oz.

    A. 2; 14   B. 2; 11   C. 2; 9   D. 2; 6

7.____

8. At the beginning of the year, a foreman has 7 dozen electric bulbs in stock. During the year, he receives a shipment of 14 dozen bulbs, and also replaces 5 burned out bulbs a month in each of 3 buildings in his area. How many electric bulbs does he have on hand at the end of the year? _____dozen.   8.____

   A. 3   B. 6   C. 8   D. 12

9. A project has 4 buildings, each 14 floors high. Each floor has 10 apartments. If 35% of the apartments in the project have 3 rooms or less, how many apartments have 4 or more rooms?   9.____

   A. 196   B. 210   C. 364   D. 406

10. An employee takes 1 hour and 30 minutes a day to sweep 30 flights of stairs. How many flights of stairs does he sweep in a month if he spends a total of 30 hours doing this job and works at the same rate?   10.____

   A. 200   B. 300   C. 600   D. 900

11. During a month, Employee A washed 30 windows, Employee B washed 4 times as many windows as Employee A, and Employee C washed half as many windows as Employee B. The TOTAL number of windows washed by all three men together during this month is   11.____

   A. 180   B. 210   C. 240   D. 330

12. How much would it cost to completely fence in the playground area shown at the right with fencing costing $7.50 a foot?   12.____
   A. $615.00
   B. $820.00
   C. $885.00
   D. $960.00

9FT.   14 FT.   26 FT.   33 FT.

13. A drill bit measures .625 inches. The fractional equivalent, in inches, is   13.____

   A. 9/16   B. 5/8   C. 11/16   D. 3/4

14. The number of cubic yards of sand required to fill a bin measuring 12 feet by 6 feet by 4 feet is MOST NEARLY   14.____

   A. 8   B. 11   C. 48   D. 96

15. Assume that you are assigned to put down floor tiles in a room measuring 8 feet by 10 feet. Individual tiles measure 9 inches by 9 inches. The total number of floor tiles required to cover the entire floor is MOST NEARLY   15.____

   A. 107   B. 121   C. 142   D. 160

16. Lumber is usually sold by the board foot, and a board foot is defined as a board one foot square and one inch thick.
If the price of one board foot of lumber is 90 cents and you need 20 feet of lumber 6 inches wide and 1 inch thick, the cost of the 20 feet of lumber is

    A. $9.00   B. $12.00   C. $18.00   D. $24.00

16.____

17. For a certain plumbing repair job, you need three lengths of pipe, 12 1/4 inches, 6 1/2 inches, and 8 5/8 inches.
If you cut these three lengths from the same piece of pipe, which is 36 inches long, and each cut consumes 1/8 inch of pipe, the length of pipe REMAINING after you have cut out your three pieces should be _____ inches.

    A. 7 1/4   B. 7 7/8   C. 8 1/4   D. 8 7/8

17.____

18. A maintenance bond for a roadway pavement is in an amount of 10% of the estimated cost.
If the estimated cost is $8,000,000, the maintenance bond is

    A. $8,000   B. $80,000   C. $800,000   D. $8,000,000

18.____

19. Specifications require that a core be taken every 700 square yards of paved roadway or fraction thereof. A 100 foot by 200 foot rectangular area would require _____ core(s).

    A. 1   B. 2   C. 3   D. 4

19.____

20. An applicant must file a map at a scale of 1" = 40'. Six inches on the map represents _____ feet on the ground.

    A. 600   B. 240   C. 120   D. 60

20.____

21. A 100' x 110' lot has an area of MOST NEARLY _____ acre.

    A. 1/8   B. 1/4   C. 3/8   D. 1/2

21.____

22. 1 inch is MOST NEARLY equal to _____ feet.

    A. .02   B. .04   C. .06   D. .08

22.____

23. The area of the triangle EFG shown at the right is MOST NEARLY _____ sq. ft.

    A. 36   B. 42   C. 48   D. 54

23.____

24. Specifications state: As further security for the faithful performance of this contract, the Comptroller shall deduct, and retain until the final payment, 10% of the value of the work certified for payment in each partial payment voucher, until the amount so deducted and retained shall equal 5% of the contract price or in the case of a unit price contract, 5% of the estimated amount to be paid to the Contractor under the contract.
For a $300,000 contract, the amount to be retained at the end of the contract is

    A. $5,000   B. $10,000   C. $15,000   D. $20,000

24.____

25. Asphalt was laid for a length of 210 feet on the entire width of a street whose curb-to-curb distance is 30 feet. The number of square yards covered with asphalt is MOST NEARLY

    A. 210   B. 700   C. 2,100   D. 6,300

25.____

KEY (CORRECT ANSWERS)

1.	C		11.	B
2.	A		12.	C
3.	B		13.	B
4.	C		14.	B
5.	B		15.	C
6.	C		16.	A
7.	B		17.	C
8.	B		18.	C
9.	C		19.	D
10.	C		20.	B

21.	B
22.	D
23.	A
24.	C
25.	B

SOLUTIONS TO PROBLEMS

1. (2)(9) = 18 man-days. Then, 18 ÷ 3 = 6 men

2. The number of employees = 1644 ÷ 2 = 822. The number of foremen needed
    = 822 ÷ 18 ≈ 45

3. 1 gallon of wax costs the same as 60 ÷ 2 = 30 bars of soap. Thus, 5 gallons of wax costs
    the same as (5)(30) = 150 bars of soap.

4. To average 280 sq.ft. for five days means a total of (5)(280) = 1400 sq.ft. for all five days.
    The number of square feet to be waxed on Friday = 1400 - (275+352+179+302) = 292

5. The acreage for buildings is 35 - 28 = 7. Then, 7/35 = 20%

6. (16)(3/4) = 12 quarts = 3 gallons. The amount of detergent, in ounces, is (2)(3) = 6. The
    amount of disinfectant is 1 oz.

7. One corn broom weighs 32 ÷ 12 = 2 2/3 lbs. ≈ 2 lbs. 11 oz.

8. Number of bulbs at the beginning of the year = (7)(12) + (14)(12) = 252. Number of bulbs
    replaced over an entire year = (5)(3)(12) = 180. The number of unused bulbs = 252 - 180
    = 72 = 6 dozen.

9. Total number of apartments = (4)(14)(10) = 560. The number of apartments with at least
    4 rooms = (.65)(560) = 364.

10. 30 ÷ 1 1/2 = 20. Then, (20)(30) = 600 flights of stairs

11. The number of windows washed by A, B, C were 30, 120, and 60. Their total is 210.

12. The two missing dimensions are 26 - 14 = 12 ft. and 33 - 9 = 24 ft. Perimeter = 9 + 12 +
    33 + 26 + 24 + 14 = 118 ft. Thus, total cost of fencing = (118)($7.50) = $885.00

13. $.625 = \dfrac{625}{1000} = \dfrac{5}{8}$

14. (12)(6)(4) = 288 cu.ft. Now, 1 cu.yd. = 27 cu.ft.; 288 cu.ft. is equivalent to 10 2/3 or about
    11 cu.yds.

15. 144 sq.in. = 1 sq.ft. The room measures (8 ft.)x(10 ft.) = 80 sq.ft. = 11,520 sq.in. Each tile
    measures (9)(9) = 81 sq.in. The number of tiles needed = 11,520 ÷ 81 = 142.2 or about
    142.

16. 20 ft. by 6 in. = (20 ft.)(1/2 ft.) = 10 sq.ft. Then, (10X.90) = $9.00

17. There will be 3 cuts in making 3 lengths of pipe, and these 3 cuts will use (3)(1/8) = 3/8
    in. of pipe. The amount of pipe remaining after the 3 pieces are removed = 36 - 12 1/4
    - 6 1/2 - 8 5/8 - 3/8 = 8 1/4 in.

18. The maintenance bond = (.10)($8,000,000) = $800,000

19. (100)(200) = 20,000 sq.ft. = 20,000 ÷ 9 ≈ 2222 sq.yds. Then, 2222 ÷ 700 ≈ 3.17. Since a core must be taken for each 700 sq.yds. plus any left over fraction, 4 cores will be needed.

20. Six inches means (6)(40) = 240 ft. of actual length.

21. (100 ft.)(110 ft.) = 11,000 sq.ft. ≈ 1222 sq.yds. Then, since 1 acre = 4840 sq.yds., 1222 sq.yds. is equivalent to about 1/4 acre.

22. 1 in. = 1/12 ft. ≈ .08 ft.

23. Area of $\triangle$ EFG = (1/2)(8)(6) + (1/2)(4)(6) = 36 sq.ft.

24. The amount to be retained = (.05)($300,000) = $15,000

25. (210)(30) = 6300 sq.ft. Since 1 sq.yd. = 9 sq.ft., 6300 sq.ft. equals 700 sq.yds.

———

TEST 2

DIRECTIONS: Each question or incomplete statement is followed by several suggested answers or completions. Select the one that BEST answers the question or completes the statement. *PRINT THE LETTER OF THE CORRECT ANSWER IN THE SPACE AT THE RIGHT.*

1. The TOTAL length of four pieces of 2" pipe, whose lengths are 7'3 1/2", 4'2 3/16", 5'7 5/16", and 8'5 7/8", respectively, is

   A. 24'6 3/4"   B. 24'7 15/16"
   C. 25'5 13/16"   D. 25'6 7/8"

   1._____

2. Under the same conditions, the group of pipes that gives the SAME flow as one 6" pipe is (neglecting friction) _____ pipes.

   A. 3 3"   B. 4 3"   C. 2 4"   D. 3 4"

   2._____

3. A water storage tank measures 5' long, 4' wide, and 6' deep and is filled to the 5 1/2' mark with water.
   If one cubic foot of water weighs 62 pounds, the number of pounds of water required to COMPLETELY fill the tank is

   A. 7,440   B. 6,200   C. 1,240   D. 620

   3._____

4. A hot water line made of copper has a straight horizontal run of 150 feet and, when installed, is at a temperature of 45°F. In use, its temperature rises to 190°F.
   If the coefficient of expansion for copper is 0.0000095" per foot per degree F, the total expansion, in inches, in the run of pipe is given by the product of 150 multiplied by 0.0000095 by

   A. 145   B. 145 x 12
   C. 145 divided by 12   D. 145 x 12 x 12

   4._____

5. To dig a trench 3'0" wide, 50'0" long, and 5'6" deep, the total number of cubic yards of earth to be removed is MOST NEARLY

   A. 30   B. 90   C. 140   D. 825

   5._____

6. If it costs $65 for 20 feet of subway rail, the cost of 150 feet of this rail will be

   A. $487.50   B. $512.00   C. $589.50   D. $650.00

   6._____

7. The number of cubic feet of concrete it takes to fill a form 10 feet long, 3 feet wide, and 6 inches deep is

   A. 12   B. 15   C. 20   D. 180

   7._____

8. The sum of 4 1/16, 51/4, 3 5/8, and 4 7/16 is

   A. 17 3/16   B. 17 1/4   C. 17 5/16   D. 17 3/8

   8._____

9. If you earn $10.20 per hour and time and one-half for working over 40 hours, your gross salary for a week in which you worked 42 hours would be

   A. $408.00   B. $428.40   C. $438.60   D. $770.80

   9._____

10. A drill bit, used to drill holes in track ties, has a diameter of 0.75 inches.   10._____
When expressed as a fraction, the diameter of this drill bit is

    A. 1/4"   B. 3/8"   C. 1/2"   D. 3/4"

11. Three dozen shovels were purchased for use.   11._____
If the shovels were used at the rate of nine a week, the number of weeks that the three dozen lasted was

    A. 3   B. 4   C. 9   D. 12

12. Assume that you earn $20,000 per year.   12._____
If twenty percent of your pay is deducted for taxes, social security, and pension, your weekly take-home pay will be MOST NEARLY

    A. $280   B. $308   C. $328   D. $344

13. If a measurement scaled from a drawing is one inch, and the scale of the drawing is 1/8   13._____
inch to the foot, then the one inch measurement would represent an ACTUAL length of

    A. 8 feet   B. 2 feet
    C. 1/8 of a foot   D. 8 inches

14. Tiles 12" x 12" are used to lay a floor having the dimensions 10'0" x 12'0".   14._____
The MINIMUM number of tiles needed to completely cover the floor is

    A. 60   B. 96   C. 120   D. 144

15. The volume of concrete in a strip of sidewalk 30 feet long by 4 feet wide by 3 inches thick   15._____
is _____ cubic feet.

    A. 30   B. 120   C. 240   D. 360

16. To change a quantity of cubic feet into an equivalent quantity of cubic yards, _____ the   16._____
quantity by _____.

    A. multiply; 9   B. divide; 9
    C. multiply; 27   D. divide; 27

17. If a pump can deliver 50 gallons of water per minute, then the time needed for this pump   17._____
to empty an excavation containing 5,800 gallons of water is _____ hour(s) _____ minutes.

    A. 2; 12   B. 1; 56   C. 1; 44   D. 1; 32

18. The sum of 3 1/6", 4 1/4", 3 5/8", and 5 7/16" is   18._____

    A. 15 9/16"   B. 16 1/8"   C. 16 23/48"   D. 16 3/4"

19. If a measurement scaled from a drawing is 2 inches, and the scale of the drawing is 1/8   19._____
inch to the foot, then the two inch measurement would represent an ACTUAL length of

    A. 8 feet   B. 4 feet
    C. 1/4 of a foot   D. 16 feet

20. A room is 7'6" wide by 9'0" long with a ceiling height of 8'0". One gallon of flat paint will 20.____
cover approximately 400 square feet of wall.
The number of gallons of this paint required to paint the walls of this room, making no
deductions for windows or doors, is MOST NEARLY

    A. 1/4   B. 1/2   C. 2/3   D. 1

21. The cost of a certain job is broken down as follows: 21.____

        Materials $3,750
        Rental of equipment   1,200
        Labor   3,150
The percentage of the total cost of the job that can be charged to materials is MOST
NEARLY

    A. 40%   B. 42%   C. 44%   D. 46%

22. By trial, it is found that by using two cubic feet of sand, a 5 cubic foot batch of concrete is 22.____
produced. Using the same proportions, the amount of sand required
to produce 2 cubic yards of concrete is MOST NEARLY _____ cubic feet.

    A. 20   B. 22   C. 24   D. 26

23. It takes 4 men 6 days to do a certain job. 23.____
Working at the same speed, the number of days it will take 3 men to do this job is

    A. 7   B. 8   C. 9   D. 10

24. The cost of rawl plugs is $27.50 per gross. The cost of 2,448 rawl plugs is 24.____

    A. $467.50   B. $472.50   C. $477.50   D. $482.50

25. In a certain district, the area of a building may be no longer than 55% of the area of the 25.____
lot on which it stands. On a rectangular lot 75 ft. by 125 ft., the maximum permissible
area of building is, in square feet, MOST NEARLY

    A. 5,148   B. 5,152   C. 5,156   D. 5,160

KEY (CORRECT ANSWERS)

1.	D		11.	B
2.	B		12.	B
3.	D		13.	A
4.	A		14.	C
5.	A		15.	A
6.	A		16.	D
7.	B		17.	B
8.	D		18.	C
9.	C		19.	D
10.	D		20.	C

21.	D
22.	B
23.	B
24.	A
25.	C

———

SOLUTIONS TO PROBLEMS

1. $3\frac{1}{6}"+4\frac{1}{4}"+3\frac{5}{8}"+5\frac{7}{16}"+=3\frac{8}{48}"+4\frac{12}{48}"+3\frac{30}{48}"+5\frac{21}{48}"=15\frac{71}{48}"=16\frac{23}{48}"$

2. The flow of a 6" pipe is measured by the cross-sectional area. Since diameter = 6", radius = 3", and so area = 9π sq.in. A single 3" pipe would have a cross-sectional area of $(3/2)\pi$ sq.in. = 2.25π sq.in. Now, $9 \div /2.25 = 4$. Thus, four 3" pipes is equivalent, in flow, to one 6" pipe.

3. (5x4x6) - (5x4x5 1/2) = 10. Then, (10)(62) = 620 pounds.

4. The total expansion = (150')(.0000095"/1 ft.)(190°-45°). So, the last factor is 145.

5. (3')(50')(5 1/2') = 825 cu.ft. Since 1 cu.yd. = 27 cu.ft., 825 cu.ft. cu.yds.

6. $150 \div 20 = 7.5$. Then, (7.5)($65) = $487.50

7. (10')(3')(1/2') = 15 cu.ft.

8. $4\frac{1}{16}+5\frac{4}{16}+3\frac{10}{16}+4\frac{7}{16}=16\frac{22}{16}=17\frac{3}{8}$

9. Gross salary = ($10.20)(40) + ($15.30)(2) = $438.60

10. $75"=\frac{75}{100}"=\frac{3}{4}"$

11. 3 dozen = 36 shovels. Then, $36 \div 9 = 4$ weeks

12. Since 20% is deducted, the take-home pay = ($20,000)(.80) = $16,000 for the year, which is $16,000 $\div$ 52 $\approx$ $308 per week.

13. A scale drawing where 1/8" means an actual size of 1 ft. implies that a scale drawing of 1" means an actual size of (1')(8) = 8'

14. (10')(12') = 120 sq.ft. Since each tile is 1 sq.ft., a total of 120 tiles will be used.

15. (30')(4')(1/4') = 30 cu.ft.

16. To convert a given number of cubic feet into an equivalent number of cubic yards, divide by 27.

17. $5800 \div 50 = 116$ min. = 1 hour 56 minutes

18. $3\frac{1}{6}"+4\frac{1}{4}"+3\frac{5}{8}"+5\frac{7}{16}"+=3\frac{8}{48}"+4\frac{12}{48}"+3\frac{30}{48}"+5\frac{21}{48}"=15\frac{71}{48}"=16\frac{23}{48}"$

19. $2 \div 1/8 = 16$, so a 2" drawing represents an actual length of 16 feet.

20. The area of the 4 walls = 2(7 1/2')(8') + 2(9')(8') = 264 sq.ft. Then, 264 ÷ 400 = .66 or about 2/3 gallon of paint.

21. $3750 + $1200 + $3150 = $8100. Then, $3750/$8100 ≈ 46%

22. 2 cu.yds. ÷ 5 cu.ft. = 54 ÷ 5 = 10.8. Now, (10.8)(2 cu.ft.) ≈ 22 cu.ft. Note: 2 cu.yds. = 54 cu.ft.

23. (4)(6) = 24 man-days. Then, 24 ÷ 3 = 8 days

24. 2448 ÷ 144 = 17. Then, (17)($27.50) = $467.50

25. (75')(125') = 9375 sq.ft. The maximum area of the building = (.55)(9375 sq.ft.) * 5156 sq.ft.

———

TEST 3

DIRECTIONS: Each question or incomplete statement is followed by several suggested answers or completions. Select the one that BEST answers the question or completes the statement. *PRINT THE LETTER OF THE CORRECT ANSWER IN THE SPACE AT THE RIGHT.*

1. A steak weighed 2 pounds, 4 ounces.
   How much did it cost at $4.60 per pound?   1.____

   A. $7.80   B. $8.75   C. $9.90   D. $10.35

2. twenty pints of water just fill a pail.
   the capacity of the pail, in gallons, is   2.____

   A. 2   B. 2 1/4   C. 2 1/2   D. 2 3/4

3. The sum of 5/12 and 1/4 is   3.____

   A. 7/12   B. 2/3   C. 3/4   D. 5/6

4. The volume of earth, in cubic yards, excavated from a trench 4'0" wide by 5'6" deep by   4.____
   18'6" long is MOST NEARLY

   A. 14.7   B. 15.1   C. 15.5   D. 15.9

5. 5/8 written as a decimal is   5.____

   A. 62.5   B. 6.25   C. .625   D. .0625

6. The number of cubic feet in a cubic yard is   6.____

   A. 9   B. 12   C. 27   D. 36

7. If it costs $16.20 to lay one square yard of asphalt, to lay a patch 15' by 15', it will cost   7.____
   MOST NEARLY

   A. $405.00   B. $3,645.00   C. $134.50   D. $243.00

8. You are assigned thirty (30) asphalt workers to be divided into two crews so that one   8.____
   crew will have 2/3 as many men as the other.
   The number of men you would put into the SMALLER crew is

   A. 10   B. 12   C. 14   D. 20

9. It takes 12 asphalt workers, working 6 hours a day, 5 days to complete a certain job.   9.____
   The number of days it will take 10 men, working 8 hours a day, to do the same job,
   assuming all work at the same rate, is

   A. 2 1/2   B. 3   C. 4 1/2   D. 6

0. A street is laid to a 3% grade.   10.____
   This means that in 150 ft., the street grade will rise

   A. 4 1/2 inches   B. 45 inches
   C. 4 1/2 feet   D. 45 feet

11. The sum of the following dimensions, 3 4/8, 4 1/8, 5 1/8, and 6 1/4, is   11._____

    A. 19   B. 19 1/8   C. 19 1/4   D. 19 1/2

12. A worker is paid $9.30 per hour.   12._____
If he works 8 hours each day on Monday, Tuesday, and Wednesday, 3 1/2 hours on
Thursday, and 3 hours on Friday, the TOTAL amount due him is

    A. $283.65   B. $289.15   C. $276.20   D. $285.35

13. The price of metal lath is $395.00 per 100 square yards. The cost of 527 square yards of   13._____
this lath is MOST NEARLY

    A. $2,076.50   B. $2,079.10   C. $2,081.70   D. $2,084.30

14. The total cost of applying 221 square yards of plaster board is $3,430.   14._____
The cost per square yard is MOST NEARLY

    A. $14.00   B. $14.50   C. $15.00   D. $15.50

15. In a three-coat plaster job, the scratch coat is 1/8 in. thick in front of the lath, the brown   15._____
coat is 3/16 in. thick, and the finish coat is 1/8 in. thick.
The TOTAL thickness of this plaster job, measured from the face of the lath, is

    A. 7/16"   B. 1/2"   C. 9/16"   D. 5/8"

16. If an asphalt worker earns $38,070 per year, his wages per month are MOST NEARLY   16._____

    A. $380.70   B. $735.00   C. $3,170.00   D. $3,807.00

17. The sum of 4 1/2 inches, 3 1/4 inches, and 7 1/2 inches is 1 foot _____ inches.   17._____

    A. 3   B. 3 1/4   C. 3 1/2   D. 4

18. The area of a rectangular asphalt patch, 9 ft. 3 in. by 6 ft. 9 in., is _____ square feet.   18._____

    A. 54   B. 54 1/4   C. 54 1/2   D. 62 7/16

19. The number of cubic feet in a cubic yard is   19._____

    A. 3   B. 9   C. 16   D. 27

20. A 450 ft. long street with a grade of 2% will have one end of the street higher than the   20._____
other end by _____ feet.

    A. 2   B. 44   C. 9   D. 20

21. If the drive wheel of a roller is 6 ft. in diameter and the tiller wheel is 4 ft. in diameter,   21._____
whenever the drive wheel makes a complete revolution on a straight pass, the tiller wheel
makes _____ revolution(s).

    A. 1   B. 1 1/4   C. 1 1/2   D. 2

22. A point on the centerline of a street is marked: Station 42 + 51. Another point on the cen-   22._____
terline 30 feet from the first is marked Station 42+81.
A third should be marked Station

    A. 12+51   B. 42+21   C. 45+51   D. 72+51

23. In twenty minutes, a truck moving with a speed of 30 miles an hour will cover a distance of _____ miles.

    A. 3   B. 5   C. 10   D. 30

23._____

24. The number of pounds in a ton is

    A. 500   B. 1,000   C. 2,000   D. 5,000

24._____

25. During his summer vacation, a boy earned $45.00 per day and saved 60% of his earnings.
If he worked 45 days, how much did he save during his vacation?

    A. $15.00   B. $18.00   C. $1,215.00   D. $22.50

25._____

KEY (CORRECT ANSWERS)

1.	D	11.	A
2.	C	12.	A
3.	B	13.	C
4.	B	14.	D
5.	C	15.	A
6.	C	16.	C
7.	A	17.	B
8.	B	18.	D
9.	C	19.	D
10.	C	20.	C

21.	C
22.	B
23.	C
24.	C
25.	C

SOLUTIONS TO PROBLEMS

1. ($4.60)(2 1/4 lbs.) = $10.35

2. 1 gallon = 8 pints, so 20 pints = 20/8 = 2 1/2 gallons

3. $\dfrac{5}{12}+\dfrac{1}{4}=\dfrac{5}{12}+\dfrac{3}{12}=\dfrac{8}{12}=\dfrac{2}{3}$

4. (4')(5 1/2')(18 1/2') = 407 cu.ft. Since 1 cu.yd. = 27 cu.ft., 407 cu.ft. $\approx$ 15.1 cu.yds.

5. 5/8=5 ÷ 8.000 = .625

6. There are (3)(3)(3) =27 cu.ft. in a cu.yd.

7. (15')(15') = 225 sq.ft. = 25 sq.yds. Then, ($16.20)(25) = $405.00

8. Let 2x = size of smaller crew and 3x = size of larger crew. Then, 2x + 3x = 30. Solving, x = 6. Thus, the smaller crew consists of 12 workers.

9. (12)(6)(5) = 360 worker-days. Then, 360 ÷ [(10)(8)] = 4 1/2 days

10. (.03)(150') = 4 1/2 ft.

11. $3\dfrac{4}{8}+4\dfrac{1}{8}+5\dfrac{1}{8}+6\dfrac{2}{8}=18\dfrac{8}{8}=19$

12. ($9.30)(8+8+8+3 1/2+3) = ($9.30)(30 1/2) = $283.65

13. The cost of 527 sq.yds. = (5.27)($395.00) = $2081.65 $\approx$ $2081.70

14. $3430 ÷ 221 $\approx$ $15.50

15. $\dfrac{1}{8}"+\dfrac{3}{16}"+\dfrac{1}{8}"=\dfrac{2}{16}"+\dfrac{3}{16}"+\dfrac{2}{16}"=\dfrac{7}{16}"$

16. $38,070 ÷ 12 = $3172.50 $\approx$ $3170.00 per month

17. 4 1/2" + 3 1/4" + 7 1/2" = 15 1/4" = 1 ft. 3 1/4 in.

18. 9 ft. 3 in. = 9 1/4 ft., 6 ft. 9 in. = 6 3/4 ft. Area = (9 1/4) (6 3/4) = 62 7/16 sq.ft.

19. A cubic yard = (3)(3)(3) = 27 cubic feet

20. (450')(.02) = 9 ft.

21. 6/4 = 1 1/2 revolutions

22. Station 42 + 51
    30 ft away would be 51 + 30 = 81 OR 51 - 30 = 21
    Station 42 + 81 or 42 + 21 (ANSWER: B)

23. 30 miles in 60 minutes means 10 miles in 20 minutes.

24. There are 2000 pounds in a ton.

25. ($45.00)(.60) = $27.00 savings per day. For 45 days, his savings is (45)($27.00) = $1215.00

———

CONSTRUCTION SAFETY AND SUPERVISION

CONTENTS

CONSTRUCTION SAFETY AND SUPERVISION

Construction work, whether it is heavy construction, light construction, or shop construction, is highly dangerous work, dangerous to both personnel and material. In accordance with official policy of conserving manpower and material, all site activities must conduct effective and continuous accident prevention programs. Operating procedures and work methods must be adopted which do not expose personnel unnecessarily to injury or occupational health hazards, or equipment and material to damage. Instruction in appropriate safety precautions must be given by all commands, and disciplinary action must be taken in any cases of willful violations or negligence.

I. SAFETY RESPONSIBILITY

The responsibility for the safety of personnel is vested in the superintendent. Since safety precautions are designed to cover usual situations in site activities, superintendent or others in authority may find it necessary to issue special precautions to their commands to cover local conditions and unusual circumstances. In addition to the posting of appropriate precautions, careful instruction and indoctrination of all personnel are necessary to ensure effective compliance.

The superintendent must require that all personnel under his jurisdiction be instructed and drilled in all applicable safety precautions, that adequate warning signs be posted in dangerous areas, and that all applicable safety precautions be observed. While he cannot delegate his final responsibility for the safety of personnel under his command, he may delegate his safety authority to the executive officer and to other subordinates.

The basic safety responsibility of supervisory personnel is to ensure that safety precautions are strictly observed and enforced in their own work areas.

Each individual is personally responsible for the strict observance of all safety precautions which are applicable to his work or duty. He must make immediate report to his superior of any unsafe condition, equipment, or material he happens to observe. He must warn any other personnel who may be endangered by any existing hazard or by any neglect of safety precautions. He must wear or use any protective clothing or equipment specified or required for the work he is doing. He must report any injury, no matter how slight, to his superior at once.

II. SAFETY ORGANIZATION

Each site is required to establish a safety organization, to develop, organize, and direct a comprehensive accident prevention program and to provide for the promulgation and enforcement of safety precautions and safe construction techniques.

SAFETY OFFICER

The safety program is usually under the direction of a SAFETY OFFICER designated by the commanding officer. The safety officer has the authority to take immediate steps to stop any operation where there is impending danger of injury to personnel or damage to equipment or material.

The safety officer lays out the safety program, after conducting job analyses and after consultations with the supervisors in charge of the various phases of construction. He maintains an adequate safety library, provides and equips safety bulletin boards, and obtains and distributes safety educational materials like posters, pamphlets, films, books, and visual aids.

He initiates and encourages activities designed to stimulate and maintain interest in safety. He cooperates with construction supervisors in the selection and placement of warning signs. He investigates and reports on all accidents, and makes recommendations with regard to the prevention or recurrences.

SUPERVISORY PERSONNEL

The safety duties of supervisory personnel are as follows:

1. They must promulgate and enforce all safety regulations.
2. They must instruct and drill their men in safe practices and provide and enforce the use of applicable personnel protective equipment.
3. They must carry out the safety recommendations of the safety officer or chief and their superiors.
4. They must caution their men repeatedly with regard to occupational hazards.
5. They must conduct regularly scheduled safety inspections in their areas of supervision.
6. They must investigate and analyze the capabilities of their men, to ensure that men are assigned to jobs which are not beyond their technical and physical capabilities.
7. They must report to their superiors at once any accidents which occur within their jurisdictions.
8. They must analyze all accidents which occur within their jurisdictions, ascertain their causes, and recommend appropriate action to prevent recurrences.
9. They must seek and follow the advice of the safety officer and of their superiors with regard to their part in the administration of the accident prevention program.

III. SAFETY PRECAUTIONS

In order to do their part in the administration of the safety program, supervisory personnel must have a thorough knowledge of the safety precautions which apply to the various types and phases of construction. Safety precautions applying to specific tools, equipment, and types of construction have been inserted in this manual. The following sections contain construction safety precautions not given elsewhere in this manual.

GENERAL SAFETY

Requirements for personnel safety are designed to cover the dangerous conditions ordinarily experienced by personnel engaged in construction and maintenance work at naval shore establishments and advanced bases. The American Standard Association Safety Code for Building Construction contains additional safety rules for the various fields of activity which constitute the building construction industry. Public works officers and others responsible for the safety of personnel employed on construction and maintenance work should have a current copy of the safety code and be familiar with its provisions.

DRINKING WATER

Fresh and pure drinking water must be supplied on every construction job. Drinking water will be obtained only from sources approved by responsible authority. Any one of the following dispensing methods should be used. Stationary bubbler with guarded orifice installed on an approved water line and fully enclosed water container and individual paper drinking cups. Also, portable sanitary drinking fountains which meet the required specifications. Dipping water out of any container by individual cup, dipper, canteen, or other utensil, is prohibited. Containers must be provided with a covering so designed and fastened as to prevent such use. All containers used to furnish drinking water must be thoroughly sterilized at least once a week, and more frequently if circumstances require, by methods approved by medical authorities.

TEMPORARY TOILET FACILITIES

For every 30 persons or less a latrine or closet space must be provided. It must be constructed so that the occupant thereof will be shielded from view and protected against the weather and falling objects. Latrines must be located so as not to contaminate any domestic water supply used for drinking purposes. They should be so located and banked that surface water cannot flood the pit. Each latrine must be provided with an adequate urinal trough. If sewers are available, connections must made at once, flush tank closets installed, and running water provided to keep the closet flushed.

At locations where neither a water carriage sewerage system nor chemical toilet is available, the latrine or closet space must contain a fly-tight box constructed over a pit latrine or over pails, or other suitable containers where pits are impracticable. Care must be taken to see that all buildings used as temporary toilets are kept in a clean and sanitary condition. The toilet seats should be scrubbed daily with soap and water, and washed off at least twice a week with an antiseptic solution.

FIRST-AID STATIONS

Where medical facilities are not available at a shore establishment a first-aid station or stations equipped with medicines and supplies common to first-aid treatment, must be established on each project at the beginning of operations and maintained for the duration of the job. On all projects employing fewer than 100 workers, 16-unit first-aid kits must be provided in the ratio of one for each 25 persons employed and these kits must be maintained with all the standard medicines and remedies.

Workmen must report all accidents, no matter how unimportant they seem to be. Minor injuries, when neglected; produce most of the infection cases. All injuries must be given first aid or medical attention immediately. First-aid care must be administered under the direction of qualified personnel.

PERSONAL PROTECTION

Chipper's goggles, welder's goggles, welder's shields, hard hats, safety shoes, rubber boots, safety belts, lifelines, life nets, life preservers or jackets, respirators, and other such protective equipment or clothing, occasioned by the type of work being done must be made available, and their use must be enforced. Personal protective equipment should be properly cleaned before being issued to personnel.

LIGHTING

Stairways, corridors, passageways, excavations, piled materials or obstructions, and working areas must be kept adequately lighted while work is in progress; and where working conditions require the use of artificial lighting it must be maintained after a shift until workmen have had an opportunity to leave the immediate area.

Outdoor operations must have adequate light for night work.

GAS AND SMOKE

No method of heating must be used which releases smoke or gas within an enclosure where workers are employed. No fire or open flame device should be permitted on a project without the approval of the supervisor or person in charge. Where smoke pipes from stoves or other heating apparatus pass through combustible walls or roof, proper insulating thimbles must be provided. All stoves and other heating apparatus must be mounted on an incombustible base and have proper fire protection at the rear and sides.

HANDLING AND STORING MATERIALS

All material in bags, containers, or bundles, and other material stored in tiers must be stacked, blocked, interlocked, and limited in height so that it will be stable and otherwise safe against sliding or collapsing.

Material stored inside buildings under construction should not be placed within 6 feet of any hoist way or floor opening, nor on any floor above the ground within 10 feet of the outside of the building, unless, the exterior walls extend above the top of the storage pile, in which case the minimum distance must be 6 feet. Material should not be stacked against interior columns or roof supports. Floors must be shored if material stored is heavier than the flooring will support. When any material is stored in public thoroughfares, it must be located so as to prevent the least possible hazard to the public or interference with traffic.

All material must be protected against being hit or knocked over by trucks or other passing vehicles by means of barricades and red flags during the hours of daylight. It should be guarded at night by barricades and an adequate number of red lights located at conspicuous points. When handling materials by hand, workmen should always use the legs in lifting, never the back. Help should be obtained if the load is too heavy or too clumsy to be handled by one man.

PILING LUMBER

Men piling lumber should always wear leather gloves. All lumber must be piled on timber sills to prevent direct contact between stored lumber and the ground. Sills must be level and solidly supported. Lumber must be so piled as to be safe against falling. The height of the pile must not exceed 16 feet. The width of piles must not be less than one-fourth the height. When unpiling, each tier must be completely unpiled before beginning another. Cross strips must be placed in piles which are stacked more than 4 feet high. Used lumber must have all projecting nails withdrawn before it is piled, unless it is burned without further handling.

CEMENT AND LIME

Men handling cement and lime bags should wear goggles and snug-fitting neck and wrist bands. Any susceptibility of their skin to cement and lime burns should be reported. They should always practice personal cleanliness. They must not wear clothing that has become hard and stiff with cement. Such clothing irritates the skin and may cause serious infection. Men who are allergic to cement and lime should be transferred to other jobs.

Bags of cement and lime should not be piled more than 10 bags high on a pallet except when stored in bins or enclosures built for such purposes. The bags around the outside of the pallet should be placed with the mouths of the bags facing the center. To prevent piled bags from falling outward, the first five tiers of bags each way from any corner must be crosspiled and a set-back made commencing with the sixth tier. If necessary to pile above the tenth tier, another set-back must be made. The back tier, when not resting against a wall of sufficient strength to withstand the pressure, should be stepped back one bag every five tiers, the same as the end tiers.

During unpiling, the entire top of the pile should be kept level and the necessary step-backs every five tiers maintained.

Lime must be stored in a dry place to prevent a premature slaking action.

BRICK

Brick should never piled directly on uneven of soft ground but should always be staked on planks. Brick must never be stored on scaffolds or runways. This must not prohibit normal supplies on bricklayers' scaffolds during actual bricklaying operations.

Except where stacked in sheds, brick piles should never be more than 7 feet high. When a pile of brick reaches a height of 4 feet it must be tapered back 1 inch in every foot of height above the 4 foot level. The tons of brick piles must be kept level and the taper maintained during unpiling operations.

MASONRY BLOCK AND HOLLOW TILE

Blocks should always be stacked in tiers on solid, level surfaces. Stacked piles should be limited to a height of 6 feet whenever possible. When blocks are stacked higher than 6 feet the pile must be stepped back, braced, and propped, or wood strips placed between tiers to prevent the pile from toppling.

Blocks should not be dropped or thrown from an elevation or delivered through fully enclosed chutes.

REINFORCING AND STRUCTURAL STEEL

Men handling reinforcing steel must wear leather gloves. Bending of reinforcing steel on the job should be done on substantial benches secured against tipping. Benches should be located on non-slippery level surfaces.

Structural steel must be carefully piled to prevent sliding or tipping over. If there is danger of tipping over, I-beams should be stored with webs horizontal.

SAND, GRAVEL, AND CRUSHED STONE

In withdrawing sand, gravel, and crushed stone from frozen stock piles, no overhang should be permitted at any time. Material should not be dumped against walls or partitions. When this must be done, it should not be stored to a height that will endanger the stability of such walls and partitions.

When men are required to work in hoppers or on high piles of loose material they must be equipped with safety belts and lifelines having no more than 2 feet of slack.

CONCRETE CONSTRUCTION

Good housekeeping must be observed at each new concrete structure. Materials and tools should be kept picked up, and special care must be taken that no boards with protruding nails are allowed to lie around. All workmen placing concrete must wear protective hats wherever the hazard of overhead falling objects exists. Shirt sleeves should be rolled down, gloves should be worn, and every reasonable precaution taken to keep cement and concrete off the skin. Men required to stand in fresh concrete should be provided with watertight boots. Men placing reinforcing steel where there is a falling hazard must be equipped with lifelines and safety belts, firmly secured with a maximum slack of 4 feet. While concreting there should be one Builder, or more if necessary, assigned to tighten wedges and to see that centering supports are not in danger of collapsing. Mud sills should be used on all shoring that rests on the ground, and shoring should be properly placed.

Before decking has been put in place on joists, temporary scaffolding should be erected as necessary to enable men to work safely. Workmen must be particularly careful not to walk out on cantilevered members of the form framing.

Men erecting column forms must always install back braces and side braces so as to prevent any movement out and away from the building. They must also use heavy tie-wire to tie in the tops of wood column forms to the slab reinforcing steel. When the outside beam forms are in place, a continuous length of 3/4-inch manila rope must run from one set of column dowels to the next set of the outside of the building. When outside column forms are being raised from one floor level to another floor level, the area below the place where the column forms are being raised should be roped off. In the setting of shores, all horizontal and cross bracing should tie in all shores with the adjacent ones.

FORM STRIPPING

Only men actually engaged in stripping work should be allowed in areas where stripping is being done. Forms should not be removed prematurely; be sure that the concrete is properly set and that it is not frozen. Before stripping, beam forms should be well supported by shoring. When large panels are removed or handled by power equipment, rope tag lines should be fastened to the form panels to prevent the wind from swinging them against the men. When tie wires under tension are being cut, care should be taken to prevent a backlash which might hit the body, especially the face, eyes, or throat. Hammer and chisel should not be used to cut tie wires.

Stripped lumber should be removed at once to a separate pile, and then cleaned and all nails removed. Workmen cleaning stripped lumber should wear heavy leather gloves and heavy soled safety shoes which are in good condition. Runways that are used for workmen's access should have standard railings on open sides to protect the workmen using them. Runways should be built with such a slope that men will not slip. Cleats should be fastened to sloping runways when the incline exceeds 1-foot rise in a 5-foot run. Runways must be kept free of loose materials, ice, snow, grease, mud, and other causes of insecure footing.

MIXING AND PLACING CONCRETE

Tools such as shovels and hoes should be placed where workmen will not trip over them or bump into them. The mortar box must be placed clear of workmen's access ways.

Workmen must make sure that the transit-mix truck does not back up and pin them between the skip and the truck, or run them down. Transit-mix truck operators must exercise special care in backing up to avoid injuring workmen. The operator should back up only on signal from qualified personnel.

Workmen must be careful not to get too near to moving parts, like revolving drums, cables, etc., thereby running the risk of their clothing being caught and drawing them into the machinery.

When a mixer dumps a load of concrete into a bucket, care must be taken to see that the bucket gate is closed. Extreme care should be taken when planning the working operations so that the bucket will not have to swing over the working men heads. Cables should be checked for defects to prevent the load being dropped.

EQUIPMENT

Operators of construction and weight-handling equipment must be tested and licensed in accordance with the applicable requirements. An apprentice or license applicant should operate equipment only under the direct supervision of a licensed operator. An operator who is not physically able or mentally alert must not be permitted to start work with any piece of equipment.

A frequent and regular inspection should be made of all machines. A well-maintained machine is usually a safe machine. All controls such as steering mechanism, brakes, and operating clutches must be tested by the operator before any work is begun on a new shift. If any of these do not operate properly, they should be adjusted or repaired before any load is moved. Good housekeeping is a prime necessity for safe and efficient operation. An accumulation of grease on a machine can cause falls and invite fires. Refueling of gasoline or diesel-operated equipment should never be done while it is in operation. Frequent inspection of fuel lines and tanks for leaks will prevent fires as well as loss of fuel.

When transporting gasoline from general supply to equipment in 5-gallon quantities, safety cans should be used. If tank truck service is not available, gasoline in quantities in excess of 5 gallons should be transported in steel drums. All bungs must be tight, and the drum itself checked for soundness. When dispensing gasoline from drums an approved pump should be used. An operator should never leave his machine while the engine is running. Upon completion of a work shift, the bucket, skip, etc., must be rested on the ground, and the brakes and clutches set as recommended by the manufacturer.

No one must ever attempt to repair, clean, oil, or grease any part of the equipment while it is in motion.

SIGNALS

One person, only, should be designated as signalman, and both he and the equipment operator should be entirely familiar with the standard hand signals. Where possible, the signalman should be given some distinguishing article of dress, such as a brightly colored helmet. He must be in a position to closely observe the load and the workmen or intermediate signalman, and still be in plain sight of the operator at all times.

CLEARING

Personal protective equipment or apparel of approved type should be worn by workers for protection against eye, head, leg, or foot injuries, and while working in water or swampy areas and on ice and other hazardous surfaces. Sharp edge tools should be transported in carrying cases or sheaths. Machetes must be kept in sheaths at all times except when in actual use. All hands should stand as far away as possible from moving machines, equipment, or moving logs and taut lines. When operations are conducted at night, adequate artificial illumination should be provided either in the form of headlights or by general lighting of the work area.

All underbrush, vines, small trees, etc., that will interfere with clearing operation, should be cleared before trimming or felling begins. Before felling, all trees must be inspected for rotten hearts, dead or entangled limbs, or similar hazardous conditions. Dead or entangling limbs which endanger personnel should be removed. Trees which present an unusual hazard, such as those with rotten heart, dead, hollow, leaning, lodged or multiple growths, should be felled under the supervision of a skilled foreman. All trees must be properly undercut before felling, with a deep "V" grooved notch on the side where the tree is to fall. Wedges should be used to throw all balanced trees. Persons in the danger areas must be warned prior to the felling of trees. A loud warning call, "TIMBER" must be given at the time of the felling of each tree.

Persons engaged in felling trees should look over the area carefully before starting to fell a tree, and note mentally the existing avenues of escape. Workmen should never climb trees while carrying unguarded sharp-edged tools. Working in or on trees during high winds is prohibited, except in an emergency, and then only under the foreman's direct supervision. After felling a tree, the tree must be lying on the ground and adequately chocked or otherwise secured before leaving it or going to the next tree. Before felled trees are trimmed, they should be properly secured by chocking or other means to prevent them from rolling. Extreme care must be exercised when using chain saws to fell trees. Chain saws must not be used to fell rotten heart or hollow trees.

BURNING

Burning operations must be kept under strict control and not left unattended. They must always be conducted in the clear, where the fire will not ignite leaves, dry wooded areas, or nearby buildings. Workmen should not stand in the smoke. All burning or smoldering material must be completely extinguished before workmen leave the scene. Firing, punching, and placing of material for burning should be done from the windward side. This is especially important when poison oak, poison sumac, or poison ivy is being burned. Workmen should never use flammable liquids on piles of material which are burning or smoldering.

POISONOUS PLANTS

If a workman has been in contact with poison ivy, poison oak, or sumac, his skin should be swabbed with alcohol and scrubbed with laundry soap and water. A brush or a rough cloth should not be used as they might irritate the skin and increase the danger of poisoning. Heavy gloves and clothing should always be worn when handling poisonous plants. The clothing of these workers should be cleaned daily. When burning poisonous vines it is important to keep away from the smoke, which will carry the poison and may be inhaled. If infection develops after contact with poisonous plants, a medical officer should be consulted. Self-medication with poisonous plant immunization or desensitization extracts should never be undertaken. Men who are extremely sensitive to these poisons should be transferred to other jobs.

EXCAVATION

Where applicable, Federal, State, or local codes, rules, regulations and ordinances governing any and all phases of excavation work should be observed at all times.

Every effort should be made prior to making an excavation to determine whether utility installations (sanitary and storm sewers, water, gas, electric lines, gasoline tanks, etc) are to be encountered. When the excavation approaches the estimated level of such an installation, the installation should be located from blueprints, if available, or by careful probing and digging, and when uncovered, it should be properly supported and protected. Trees, boulders, and other surface encumbrances located so as to create a hazard at any time during operations must be removed before excavation is started.

If the stability of adjoining buildings or walls is endangered by, excavations, necessary shoring, bracing, or underpinning must be proved to ensure their safety. Such shoring, bracing, or underpinning should be frequently inspected by a competent person and the protection effectively maintained. If it is necessary to place or operate power shovels, derricks, trucks, material, or other heavy objects on a level above and near an excavation, the side of the excavation must be sheet-piled, shored, and braced as necessary to resist the extra pressure due to such superimposed loads. Wherever any side of an excavation is a masonry wall, such wall should be braced to ensure stability. This should not include reinforced concrete walls known to be of ample strength. Temporary sheet piling which has been installed to permit the construction of a retaining wall must not be removed until such wall has acquired its full strength.

Except in hard rock, excavations below the level of the base or footing of any foundation or retaining wall should not be permitted unless the wall is underpinned and all other precautions taken to ensure the stability of the adjacent walls for the protection of the workmen. Undercutting of earth banks should not be permitted unless they are adequately shored. Excavations should be inspected after every rain storm or other hazard-increasing occurrence, and the protection against slides and cave-ins increased if necessary. All fixed-in-place ladders and stairways giving access to levels 20 or more feet apart should be provided with landing platforms at vertical intervals of not more than 20 feet. Every landing platform should be equipped with standard railings and toe boards.

JACKS

Workmen should always select the proper size jack for the load to be lifted. A jack of too light capacity can strip itself, releasing the load; and a jack with too little height will run itself out before accomplishing the purpose intended. The jack should be inspected before using. If there is any doubt about the jack's condition, it should not be used. The base of the jack should be placed on a level firm footing where it cannot slip or kick away. When the object has been lifted to the desired height, blocking or cribbing must be immediately placed under it.

TRENCHES

Particular attention should be given to shoring of trenches, especially if there are roadways or railroad lines in the vicinity of the excavation or if men are to work in the trench. In the following paragraphs, provisions for shoring and bracing of excavations should apply, except when the full depth of the excavation is in stable solid rock, hard slag, or hard shale or the shoring plan has been designed by the engineering office.

The sides of excavations 4 feet or more in depth, or in which the soil is so unstable that it is not considered safe at lesser depths, should be supported by substantial and adequate sheeting, sheet piling, bracing, shoring, etc., or the sides sloped to the angle of repose. Surface areas adjacent to the sides should be well drained. Trenches in partly saturated, filled, or unstable soils should be suitably braced.

Excavated or other material must not be stored nearer than 2 feet from the edge of a trench. In the case of extremely deep trenches, material should be stored farther away than 2 feet. The safe storage distance is in proportion to the depth of the trench; the deeper the trench the farther away the material should be stored. Where pedestrian and vehicular traffic is to be maintained over, or adjacent to excavations, proper safeguards should be provided, such as walkways, bridges, guardrails, barricades, warning flags, lights, or illumination,

Where an excavation is close to a cut, particularly when nearer to the cut than its depth, special shoring should be used. Men working in deep trenches should wear hard hats as a protection against falling material. Access to excavations over 5 feet deep should be by ramps, ladders, stairways, or hoists. Workmen should not jump into the trench, nor use the bracing as a stairway.

No tools, materials, or debris should be left on walkways, ramps, struts, or near the edge of an excavation. Such material might be knocked off or cause a worker to lose his footing. Pick-and-shovel men working in trenches must keep sufficient distance apart so they cannot injure each other when working with their shovels.

Extra care should be used in excavating around gas mains, oil tanks, gasoline or oil pipe lines, etc. Smoking or open fires of any kind are prohibited in areas where gaseous conditions are suspected. In such places the air should be tested and, if gas is present, ventilation should be provided by portable blowers or other satisfactory methods. Workmen should put up barricades and lights around the excavation at the end of each work shift for the safety of personnel moving in that area after dark.

EYE HAZARDS

Many operations in an industrial facility involve eye hazards. Certain areas, machines and trades are therefore required to be designated as "eye-hazardous." These include, but are not limited to such operations as arc-welding, the handling of acids, and grinding, chipping and other machining processes which are accompanied by the generation of flying particles.

In order to afford a measure of protection to the casual uniformed visitor, areas and machines which have been designated as "eye-hazardous" should be permanently screened and permanently marked with a black and yellow checkerboard symbol and the phrase, EYE HAZARD, in black on a yellow background. Other areas where personnel are involved in eye-hazardous occupations should be clearly marked with portable screens and signs with the same markings.

Signs similar to the portable sign should be placed on the outside of buildings which are entirely occupied by eye-hazardous processes. These signs should be placed on the door in every case and beside the door if space permits. If space does not permit, the sign beside the door can be replaced by a black and yellow checkerboard which extends from 3 feet above the sill to 7 feet above the sill on both door jambs. Large or multiple doors should have the sign repeated at about 6 foot intervals or repeated on each door, whichever is appropriate. Welding sets in general should be clear blue as for electrical controls. Compressors, generators and other miscellaneous machinery should be painted medium gray.

FLAMMABLE LIQUIDS

Red has been traditionally used on containers for kerosene, gasoline, naphtha, alcohol, solvents and other flammable liquids. This practice is obviously wrong because of conflict with the use of red on fire protection devices. For safety and better visibility, safety cans, small portable tanks and drums used for storage and transportations of gasoline within establishments should be painted brilliant yellow throughout and should have the contents conspicuously marked with large black letters. On large fixed tanks, medium gray may be used for the body, with a large area of yellow added with black letters indicating contents.

IV. SAFETY PRECAUTIONS FOR PORTABLE POWER TOOLS

Portable power tools should be kept cleaned, oiled, and repaired. They should be carefully inspected before use. The switches must operate properly and the cords are clean and free of defects. The plug should be clean and sound.

The casings of all electrically driven tools should be grounded. Double insulated tools from sources qualified under the applicable specification are exempt from this grounding requirement.

Sparking portable electric tools should not be used where flammable vapors; gases, liquids, or exposed explosives are present.

Care should be taken that cords do not come in contact with sharp objects; they should not be allowed to kink, nor left where they might be run over. Cords must not come in contact with oil or grease, hot surfaces, or chemicals. Damaged cords should be replaced. They are not to be patched with tape. Tools should be stored in a clean, dry place where the cord can be loosely coiled.

POWER TWIST DRILLS

A portable power drill should be grasped firmly during the operation to prevent it from bucking or breaking loose, thereby causing injury or damage. When the work is completed, the drills should be removed, and drill and motor should both be well cleaned.

PNEUMATIC TOOLS

Builders using this type of tool should wear and use necessary protective devices. Only authorized and trained Builders should operate pneumatic tools. Persons with arthritis, neuritis, or circulatory disease should not use vibrating tools such as hammers, chisels, tempers, riveters, or corkers.

When not in use pneumatic tools should be laid down in such a manner that no harm can be done if the switch is accidentally tripped. No idle tool should be left in a standing position. It should be kept in good operating condition, thoroughly inspected at regular intervals with particular attention given to control and exhaust valves, hose connections, guide clips on hammers, and the chucks of reamers and drills.

The valve should be closed and the air exhausted from the line through the pneumatic tool being used before disconnecting the line from the tool. The air hose should be suitable to withstand the pressure required for the tool. Leaking or defective hose should be removed from service. Hose should not be laid over ladders, steps, scaffolds, or walkways in such a manner as to create a tripping hazard. Where hose is run through doorways, the hose should be protected against damage by the door edge.

Compressed air should not be used to clean clothing being worn or to blow dust off the body. An air hose should never be pointed at other persons.

Pneumatic Rock Drills

Under no circumstances should the operator of portable pneumatic drills wear loose or torn clothing. Only trained competent Builders, wearing necessary protective devices, should operate drills.

Bits should be examined for defects; particular attention should be paid to bit flutes which should be ground to uniform size, sharpness, and length. The machine should be held on a straight line with the hole being bored. Tipping of bit is prohibited. The machine should not be fed too fast.

The operator should be on firm footing before commencing operation. All drills should be equipped with a hand-grip switch that will shut off the supply of air when grip is released. This switch should not be modified or bypassed.

Pneumatic Paving Breakers

Suitable goggles should be worn when operating pneumatic paving breakers to protect the eyes from flying particles.

Operators must make sure that the breaker and its accessories are in good working condition. When air is used for power, the valves and connections should be checked carefully. Also, when laying down this pneumatic tool, the operator must be careful to see that the trigger cannot be operated accidentally.

When shock tools are re-dressed the heads should not be tempered, since hard heads will spall and are more dangerous than those which mushroom.

Pneumatic paving breaker operators should never cut off the air supply to the machine by purposely kinking the hose while disconnecting this equipment. Air should be cut off at the source. If the job is near a sidewalk or other thoroughfare, canvas barriers or other suitable screens should be placed on either side to protect others from flying particles.

When using a paving breaker to break up extremely hard materials such as heavy blocks embedded in concrete slabs or with hard and slick surfaces that may cause the tool to slip around instead of biting into the surface, Builders should first use a sledge hammer to roughen the surface. This practice will guard against breaking or cutting the legs or feet.

Power Hammers

No Builder should point any pneumatic hammer at other Builders. Hammers should be operated in a careful and safe manner at all times. All hammers should be equipped with a device for holding the tool in the machine. These safety tool holders should be inspected at frequent intervals.

The operator of a power hammer should not restrict the air exhaust port in any fashion. All pneumatic hammers should be equipped with a hand-grip safety switch. The pneumatic hammer should be used only for those purposes for which intended.

All hammer operators should wear necessary eye, face, and body protection. Operators of pneumatic hammers should wear gloves.

Power Wrenches

Pneumatic wrench operators should use a wrench only for those purposes for which it is intended. All wrenches should be equipped with hand-grip safety switches. All wrenches should be inspected frequently by a competent Builder. Operators of pneumatic wrenches should not wear loose fitting articles of clothing. Wrench operators should use all protective devices provided.

POWER ACTUATED TOOLS

Powder actuated tools should be operated, repaired, serviced, and handled only by Builders who have been trained and certified by the manufacturer, his authorized representative, or Department certified instructors. In applications to concrete, approval for use of the tool should be given only after it has been ascertained that it will give satisfactory results and create no spalling or "shelling-out."

Each powder-actuated tool to be used at the work site will be presented to the designated representative for inspection and registration. If acceptable, a tool permit will be issued prior to use at the work site. For each powder-actuated tool registered, the following data will be obtained and recorded: trade name; manufacturer; model and size; serial number; ownership. The use of powder-actuated tools in explosive or flammable atmospheres is prohibited.

The tool operator, together with other personnel in the vicinity, should wear safety goggles or other approved safety-type face and eye protective devices and a hard hat. Powder-actuated tools and the powder charges will be secured to prevent unauthorized possession. Upon the detection of any defect in the operation of a powder-actuated tool, the tool will be removed from service until the deficiency is corrected. Powder-actuated, fastener-type tools which, by means of a powder charge propellant, discharge an object for the purpose of affixing it to or penetrating another object, should meet the following requirements:

The muzzle end of the tool, including barrel extensions, should have a protective shield or guard at least 3 inches in diameter, securely attached, perpendicular to the barrel, designed to confine the flying particles and arrest the ricochet of the projectiles; or, in lieu of such shield or guard, a jig providing equivalent protection may be used. The tool should be made incapable of firing if not equipped with either a standard guard or a special guard, fixture, or jig of the manufacturer's design. The tool should not be operated against other than a flat work surface unless it is equipped with a special head or jig to accommodate the curvature of the surface. The tool should be so designed that it will not operate, when equipped with the standard guard indexed to the center position, if the bearing surface of the guard is tilted more than eight degrees from contact with the work surface.

Fasteners should not be driven directly into materials such as brick or concrete closer than 3 inches from the edge or corner, or into steel surfaces closer than one-half inch from the edge or corner, unless a special guard, fixture, or jig is used. Penetration must not endanger personnel, equipment, materials, or surroundings on the opposite side of the object to which the fastener is being affixed.

All powder-actuated tools and their use should comply with such Federal, State and local laws as are applicable.

POWER SAWS

In addition to the general precautions for portable electrical and pneumatic tools contained in this chapter, the precautions common to both electrical and pneumatic portable saws are as follows:

All circular portable power saws should be provided with guards that fully encompass the unused portion of the blades.

Circular saw blades should be installed by a qualified Builder and only when the source of power is disconnected from the tool.

Only a hand grip switch, electric or pneumatic, should be used.

Never use a blade which has a speed rating less than the saw on which it is being used. If the saw begins to "lug down," back it out slowly and firmly in a straight line.

V. SAFETY PRECAUTIONS FOR ASPHALT AND CONCRETE EQUIPMENT

Where safety precautions are considered to be necessary but have not been provided, or where existing precautions are judged to be inadequate, the Builder in charge will issue new or supplementary precautions that are deemed necessary for the protection of personnel and property. Listed below are some specific rules for asphalt and concrete equipment.

ASPHALT EQUIPMENT

Paint, or otherwise mark, pipes through which heated asphalt is flowing. Bare skin contact with such lines may result in severe burns. Place heating devices, such as the asphalt melter, on a level, firm foundation and protect it against traffic, accidental tipping, or similar hazards. Provide adequate fire extinguishers at the location of heating devices.

Allow hot equipment, such as the aggregate dryer, to cool sufficiently before attempting to clean or otherwise maintain it.

Maintain a minimum 3-inch covering of asphalt over the top of heating tubes when heating asphalt in equipment that utilizes an open flame heating system. Perform all heating in a level, well-ventilated area, with the item of equipment in which the asphalt is being heated at a halt. Make sure fire extinguishers are on hand and properly charged in the event of fire.

When dedrumming or heating asphalt cement, do not smoke or use open flames within 50 feet of the equipment. When heating, de-drumming, or manufacturing asphalt cutbacks, extend this distance to 100 feet.

Do not climb on equipment or stand on aggregate stockpiles in bins while equipment is in operation.

Do not use open flames around asphalt or fuel storage tanks.

Do not stand between the asphalt finisher and haul trucks.

CONCRETE EQUIPMENT

Keep the area beneath batching plants as free of personnel as possible. Be sure that men operating haul equipment have left their vehicles before commencing batching.

Empty batching plants before attempting repairs. Work on fully or partially loaded plants must be carried out only in cases of extreme urgency.

Guard against the possibility of shock when undertaking to maintain such electrically powered apparatus as the central mix plant or the slip-form paver by ensuring that they are shut down and by using only approved insulated tools.

Wear hard hats around the batch and central mix plants.

VI. BUTANE OR BLOWTORCH SAFETY

Every blowtorch should be provided with a complete set of operating instructions (i.e., directions for filling, pumping up the air pressure, lighting, and extinguishing), and no one should use a blowtorch until he has read and is familiar with the operating instructions.

The blowtorch should, preferably, be filled out-of-doors. If it is filled indoors, it should be filled at a point remote from open flame, sparks, or other source of ignition. The torch should not be filled while hot. Safety cans should be used when blowtorches are being filled. Gasoline containing lead compounds or benzol should not be used.

Laundry soap may be used on threads of the filler plug to ensure a tight seal. The filler plug should be tightened gently; force may ruin the gasket or strip the threads of the plug. The filler plug should not be loosened while the burner is hot.

Alterations on torches which would permit pumping up the pressure by any method other than the use of pumping devices provided by the torch manufacturers should not be made. No device other than the pump supplied with the torch should be used to obtain working pressure. Preferably, pressure should not be pumped up while the torch is lighted. Torches should not at any time be pumped up to excessive pressure. Five to fifteen strokes of the pump are enough, depending upon the size of the tank and the amount of gasoline in it.

Before torches are stored the pressure in the tanks should be released and the valves secured. Before torches are lighted they should be examined carefully for leaks. All torches should be inspected and tested at frequent and regular intervals by a competent Builder to make sure that the torches are in proper operating condition. Any defect found in torches should be reported at once to the supervisor. No torch which is defective in any way should be used until after such defect has been properly repaired.

The priming cup should not be overfilled, as the gasoline may flow over the tank and become ignited, thus furnishing sufficient heat to develop a dangerous pressure within the tank. If gasoline should flow over the tank it should be carefully wiped off before the torch is lighted. When heating tile, care should be taken to prevent igniting of the material being heated.

Torches should not be lighted until the gasoline in the priming cup has nearly all been consumed. Immediately after the torch has been lighted the flame should be shielded from the wind. Windbreaks should be made of noncombustible material, without bottoms and easily removable. Torches should preferably be preheated and lighted out-of-doors.

Stuffing boxes should be kept tight so as to prevent leaks around the valve stem. They should not be tightened while torches are in use.

A torch should not be used in a small unventilated space. It may heat up and thus become a source of danger, and it may exhaust the supply of oxygen, causing the operator to lose consciousness or even his life from suffocation. When such use is unavoidable, it is necessary to provide air fed respiratory protective equipment for the workers. Torches should not be dragged across the floor or abused in any other way.

Torches fired with petroleum gases are preferred to those fired by gasoline because of the fewer hazards. However, liquefied petroleum gases, which are composed of propane, propylene, butane, or butylene, present a hazard comparable to that of any flammable natural of manufactured gas and in addition they are heavier than air. Therefore, there must be adequate ventilation of spaces in which the gas is used. Precautions should be taken to assure that control valves are tightly closed after use and that there are no leaky valves or connections.

VII. SAFETY HOUSEKEEPING

Good housekeeping in working areas is as important to safety as it is to efficiency. Beside the idea of "a place for everything and everything in its place," good housekeeping includes the matter of keeping working areas and thoroughfares clear of rubbish, debris, nonessential articles, and the like, which tend to create tripping and/or fire hazards.

OUTDOOR HOUSEKEEPING

To reduce fire hazard, any natural growth on an area which is to be used for the storage of lumber or other combustible material must be burned off or otherwise cleared before material is stored in the area. A margin 50 ft. wide should be cleared beyond the outer boundaries of the area.

To reduce fire hazard, crawl spaces must be kept clear of vegetation and debris, and they must not be used for the storage of combustible material. A margin at least 50 ft. wide should be cleared, and kept clear, beyond the outer boundaries of any structure.

Waste flammable liquids must not be poured into sewers or drains. They should be collected in steel drums or other fireproof receptacles and disposed of as recommended by the safety officer. Definite areas for the dumping of refuse must be set aside and plainly identified, and refuse must not be dumped or allowed to accumulate anywhere else.

All thoroughfares must be kept clear. Ice or snow must be removed at once if possible. If not, slipperiness must be reduced by spreading gritty material, such as sand, gravel, or ashes. On any structure where a water hazard exists, life rings must be provided at intervals of not more than 200 ft. All men working over the water must be provided with life jackets, and the jackets must be worn.

All outdoor traffic hazards, such as stock piles, excavations, low overhangs, and the like must be marked with suitable warning signs, flags, barricades, lights, for other markers.

INDOOR HOUSEKEEPING

All working spaces, construction areas, and repair areas must be regularly policed, to maintain order and cleanliness and to eliminate tripping and fire hazards.

All indoor traffic hazards, such as stock piles, floor openings, low overhangs, changes in floor level, and the like must be barricaded or marked with suitable warning signs.

All rubbish, scrap material, and the like must be placed in appropriate identified receptacles. All working areas must be kept clear of rubbish and scrap, and all such material must be removed from structures at least once a day. Oily rags, steel wool, waste paper, and other flammable waste materials must be placed in tightly closed fireproof containers, and the contents of these containers must be disposed of, as recommended by the safety officer, at the end of each working day.

Ample and well-defined thoroughfares should be laid out in structures, and traffic should be confined to them as much as possible. Thoroughfares must be kept clear of obstructions and debris. Collision hazards at blind corners should be eliminated by the installation of mirrors. Running, which is often the cause of slipping, tripping, and collision accidents, must be prohibited. Floors and decks must be kept free of protruding nails, splinters, holes, and loose boards.

Stairway openings must be guarded by railings not less than 36 in. or more than 42 in. above the floor surface. A stairway between 22 and 44 in. wide must have at least one handrail. A stairway over 44 in. but less than 88 in. wide must have a handrail on each side. A stairway 88 in. wide or wider must have a handrail on each side and another down the center. Handrails must not be less than 30 in. nor more than 34 in. high, as measured from the top of a tread at the face of a riser.

Stairways must be kept well lighted, clean, dry, and free of slippery substances, refuse, and obstructions. There must be no storage of materials on stairways.

VIII. SUPERVISION

As a Builder, you must know and observe all safety precautions for the equipment you use and the work you do. In addition, it is your responsibility to ensure that all men working under your supervision also observe the proper safety rules. You must make certain, for instance, that every man in the shop knows the location of the portable firefighting equipment and that he knows how to use it.

There are dozens of precautions that must be observed; make frequent checks to see that they are. When you are giving your men instructions, either formally or informally, teach safety as an integral part of the program. Follow all applicable safety precautions.

Accident prevention is both a science and an art. It represents, above all other things, control—scientific control of personnel performance, machine performance, and physical environment. From the standpoint of handling people so that they willingly work safely, accident prevention is an art.

Safety plays a major role in any supervisory job and, to a considerable degree, affects the supervisor's ability to meet the demands required of him.

The attitude of the supervisor influences the attitudes of his men. When a supervisor has the attitude that safety does not pay, he can be sure that his men will ignore safety. When a supervisor is safety-conscious, his men will be safety-conscious. If you are one of the few supervisors who think that safety is unimportant, consider how you would feel if one of your men were injured or killed because of your negligence. Would you want it on your conscience? Could you face the family of the man?

SAFETY EDUCATION

Many supervisors feel that it is only necessary to provide safeguards and safety will then take care of itself. Provision of safeguards is a move in the right direction, but it alone will not get good results. To maintain a good safety record, the supervisor needs to employ a combination of safety devices and safety training. If each man has had sound safety training, he will be able to guard against even those hazards where safety devices are impracticable. The supervisor must, however, train every man in the use of safeguards, explaining why, as well as how, they should be used. How many supervisors have seen a man shut off the power on a machine and then walk away from it before it has stopped turning? Such a man uses a safeguard, but he does not know why he uses it. By providing the necessary training, an alert supervisor will make sure that such careless uses of safeguards do not happen again.

Standup safety meetings should be held in every shop once every week. The meetings should be held at or near the work place. Instead of a routine safety lecture, it is much better to hold a group discussion of specific accidents that are to be guarded against or that may have happened in the unit. The men should be encouraged to express their ideas. A group conclusion as to how specific accidents can be prevented should be reached.

Another type of safety meeting is one in which the supervisor presents a safety problem that has developed because of new work or new equipment. Again, the men should be invited to express their ideas.

A third type of safety meeting is one in which actual demonstrations and practice by the group is carried out. You might demonstrate how to lift, and then have the men practice lifting. Also, to make the reasons for lifting in this manner more realistic, a little lesson on the classes of tools and a little problem in ratio and proportion should prove interesting.

If you are demonstrating how to use a saw, bring in a saw and use it—don't just talk about how to use it. Then, again, let the men practice.

Making these meetings interesting is of the utmost importance. The supervisor should not complain or scold, and the meetings should be limited in time. The subject should be thought out carefully in advance and it should be timely. Considerable ingenuity is required to keep these meetings from degenerating into dull, routine affairs. Some supervisors have the men themselves rotate as leaders of the safety meetings—an excellent device to maintain interest. Hundreds of good motion pictures and other visual aids are available on safety subjects. Use them.

ACCIDENT REPORTING

When an accident occurs in your shop, office, or within your crew, you must fill out a department al Accidental Injury/Death Report. This form provides a method of recording the essential facts concerning an accident, from which data for use in accident prevention can be compiled. "Corrective action taken/recommended"—is the most important part of this report. The manner in which this question is answered provides a clue to the attitude of the supervisor.

Too many supervisors answer this question with, "The man has been warned to be more careful." This type of answer does not mean a thing. The answer to this question should tie in with the rest of the report. If an unsafe condition is the cause of the accident, you cannot correct it by warning the man to be more careful. Study the report; analyses it; then take the proper corrective action. This report is one of your best accident prevention tools if properly used. In many cases the difference between a minor accident and a major one is a matter of luck. Do not ignore the small cuts and bruises; investigate the reasons for them and correct the causes. If you do this, you will have a safe shop or office and an efficient one.

ACCIDENT INVESTIGATION

To fill out an accident report properly you must know that an accident investigation must be conducted. Here are six important factors you should consider:

1. Unsafe conditions. Was the equipment improperly guarded, unguarded, inadequately guarded? Was the equipment or material rough, slippery, sharp-edged, decayed, worn, cracked? Was there a hazardous arrangement, such as congested work space, lack of proper lifting equipment, unsafe planning? Was there proper illumination, ventilation? Was the man dressed properly for the job? Was he provided with the proper respirator goggles/ gloves?

2. Type of Accident. Was he struck by some object? Did he fall at the same level or to a different level? Was he caught in or between objects? Did he slip (not fall) or overexert himself?

3. Unsafe Act. Was he operating a machine without authority? Was he working at an un-safe speed, too fast or too slow? Was any safety device made inoperative (for example, blocked out or removed)? Was any load made unsafe, or were tools or equipment put in an unsafe place where they would fall? Did someone fail to wipe up oil, water, grease, paint, etc., on working surfaces? Did the injured man take an unsafe position of posture? Did he lift with a bent back or while in an awkward position? Did he lift jerkily? Was he riding in an unsafe position on a vehicle? Was he using improper means of ascending or descending? Was the injury caused by failure to wear the provided safe attire or personal protective devices such as goggles, gloves, masks, aprons, safety shoes?

4. Unsafe Personal Factor. Was he absentminded or inattentive? Did he fail to understand instructions, regulations, and safety rules? Did he willfully disregard instructions or safety rules? Was he unaware of safe practices, unpracticed, unskilled? Was he unable to recognize or appreciate the hazard? Did he have a bodily defect, such as poor eyesight, defective hearing, and hernia?

5. Type of Injury. Did he sustain a cut, bruise, sprain, strain, hernia, fracture? Generally you should get this information from a doctor, because it is often difficult for a layman to diagnose injuries.

6. Part of Body Affected. Did the injury involve arm, leg, ribs, feet, fingers, head, etc.? This information should also be obtained from the doctor.

The factors cited above will give you an idea of some of the things which a supervisor must investigate and report when accidents occur. It is not all-inclusive. Each accident is different, and each should be investigated and judged on its merits. Do not jump to conclusions. Start each investigation with an open mind. The most important factor in any accident investigation is to determine how to prevent a similar accident.

PLANNING

The planning of day to day assignments for team/work crews can be a frustrating job unless the crew leaders are familiar with the capabilities of his men and equipment needed to complete the work projects assigned. This is particularly true in a combat zone where the priorities of construction may change every day. You may have your best team/work crew on a prefabricating project when suddenly an emergency comes up that requires your team/ work crews plus a good portion of equipment to be dispatched to another jobsite. Since the project has to be completed, you must be able to re-organize and assign team/work crews to continue work on the original project. By knowing your men and their capabilities you should be able to control the various projects and:

1. Plan work to avoid wasted or poorly utilized manpower.

2. Be sure that each element in a project is really necessary. Eliminate or combine operations.

3. Arrange priorities of projects and have second or third projects ready so that a crew can shift work if delayed on a primary project.

4. Make sure tools, supplies, and materials are on hand.

5. Distinguish types of manpower required for different projects.

6. Establish rate of work. How many hours should a particular project take under normal conditions, and under adverse conditions.

The above points are necessary for getting the project finished; as well as aiding you in controlling the project operations. Never forget these three words—ORGANIZE, SUPERVISE and ANALYZE.

BASIC FUNDAMENTALS OF
DRAWINGS AND SPECIFICATIONS

A building project may be broadly divided into two major phases: (1) the DESIGN phase, and (2) the CONSTRUCTION phase. In accordance with a number of considerations, of which the function and desired appearance of the building are perhaps the most important, the architect first conceives the building in his mind's eye, as it were, and then sets his concept down on paper in the form of PRESENTATION drawings. Presentation drawings are usually done in PERSPECTIVE, by employing the PICTORIAL drawing techniques.

Next the architect and the engineer, working together, decide upon the materials to be used in the structure and the construction methods which are to be followed. The engineer determines the loads which supporting members will carry and the strength qualities the members must have to bear the loads. He also designs the mechanical systems of the structure, such as the lighting, heating, and plumbing systems. The end-result of all this is the preparation of architectural and engineering DESIGN SKETCHES. The purpose of these sketches is to guide draftsmen in the preparation of CONSTRUCTION DRAWINGS.

The construction drawings, plus the SPECIFICATIONS to be described later, are the chief sources of information for the supervisors and craftsman responsible for the actual work of construction. Construction drawings consist mostly of ORTHOGRAPHIC views, prepared by draftsmen who employ the standard technical drawing techniques, and who use the symbols and other designations

You should make a thorough study of symbols before proceeding further with this chapter. Figure 1 illustrates the conventional symbols for the more common types of material used on structures. Figure 2 shows the more common symbols used for doors and windows.

Before you can interpret construction drawings correctly, you must also have some knowledge of the structure and of the terminology for common structural members.

I. STRUCTURES

The main parts of a structure are the LOAD-BEARING STRUCTURAL MEMBERS, which support and transfer the loads on the structure while remaining in equilibrium with each other. The places where members are connected to other members are called JOINTS. The sum total of the load supported by the structural members at a particular instant is equal to the total DEAD LOAD plus the total LIVE LOAD.

The total dead load is the total weight of the structure, which gradually increases, of course, as the structure rises, and remains constant once it is completed. The total live load is the total weight of movable objects (such as people, furniture, bridge traffic or the like) which the structure happens to be supporting at a particular instant.

The live loads in a structure are transmitted through the various load-bearing structural members to the ultimate support of the earth as follows. Immediate or direct support for the live loads is provided by HORIZTONAL members; these are in turn supported by VERTICAL members; which in turn are supported by FOUNDATIONS and/or FOOTINGS; and these are, finally, supported by the earth.

The ability of the earth to support a load is called the SOIL BEARING CAPACITY; it is determined by test and measured in pounds per square foot. Soil bearing capacity varies considerably with different types of soil, and a soil of given bearing capacity will bear a heavier load on a wide foundation or footing than it will on a narrow one.

VERTICAL STRUCTURAL MEMBERS

Vertical structural members are high-strength columns; they are sometimes called PILLARS in buildings. Outside wall columns and inside bottom-floor columns, usually rest directly on footings. Outside-wall columns usually extend from the footing or foundation to the roof line. Inside bottom-floor columns extend upward from footings or foundations to horizontal members which in turn support the

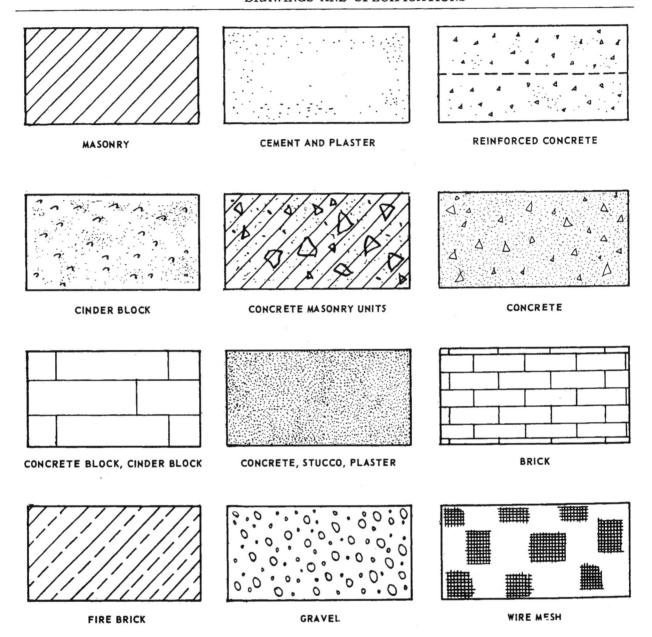

Figure 1.—Material symbols.

first floor. Upper floor columns usually are located directly over lower floor columns.

A PIER in building construction might be called a short column. It may rest directly on a footing, or it may be simply set or driven in the ground. Building piers usually support the lowermost horizontal structural members.

In bridge construction a pier is a vertical member which provides intermediate support for the bridge superstructure.

The chief vertical structural members in light frame construction are called STUDS. They are supported on horizontal members called SILLS or SOLE PLATES, and are topped by horizontal members called TOP PLATES or RAFTER PLATES. CORNER POSTS are enlarged studs, as it were, located at the building corners. In early FULL-FRAME construction a corner post was usually a solid piece of larger timber. In most modern construction BUILT-UP

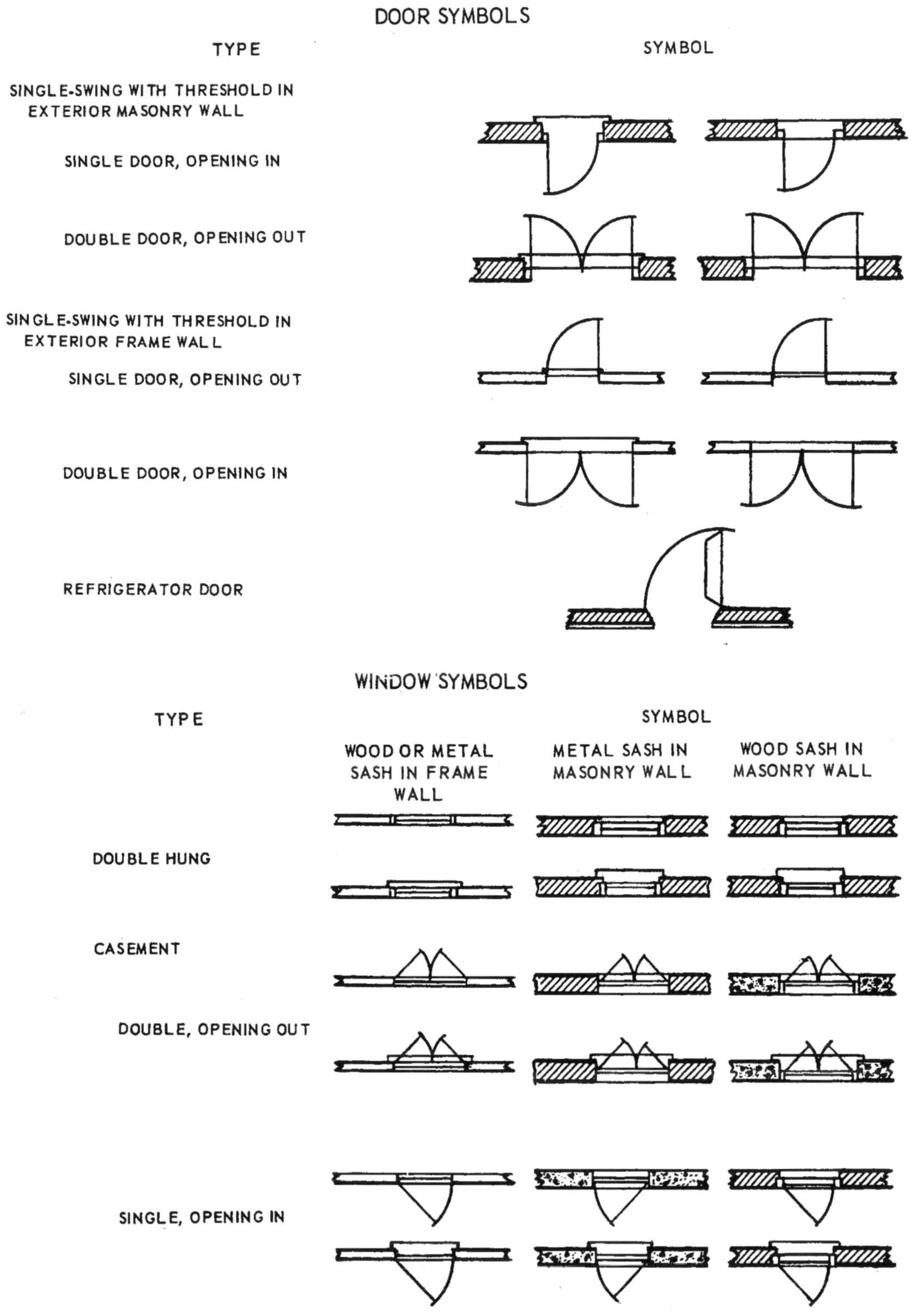

DOOR SYMBOLS

TYPE	SYMBOL
SINGLE-SWING WITH THRESHOLD IN EXTERIOR MASONRY WALL	
SINGLE DOOR, OPENING IN	
DOUBLE DOOR, OPENING OUT	
SINGLE-SWING WITH THRESHOLD IN EXTERIOR FRAME WALL	
SINGLE DOOR, OPENING OUT	
DOUBLE DOOR, OPENING IN	
REFRIGERATOR DOOR	

WINDOW SYMBOLS

TYPE	SYMBOL		
	WOOD OR METAL SASH IN FRAME WALL	METAL SASH IN MASONRY WALL	WOOD SASH IN MASONRY WALL
DOUBLE HUNG			
CASEMENT			
DOUBLE, OPENING OUT			
SINGLE, OPENING IN			

Figure 2 —Architectural symbols (door and windows).

corner posts are used, consisting of various numbers of ordinary studs, nailed together in various ways.

HORIZONTAL STRUCTURAL MEMBERS

In technical terminology, a horizontal load-bearing structural member which spans a space, and which is supported at both ends, is called a BEAM. A member which is FIXED at one end only is called a CANTILEVER. Steel members which consist of solid pieces of the regular structural steel shapes are called beams, but a type of steel member which is actually a light truss is called an OPEN-WEB STEEL JOIST or a BAR STEEL JOIST.

Horizontal structural members which support the ends of floor beams or joists in wood frame construction are called SILLS, GIRTS, or GIRDERS, depending on the type of framing being done and the location of the member in the structure. Horizontal members which support studs are called SILL or SOLE PLATES. Horizontal members which support the wall-ends of rafters are called RAFTER PLATES. Horizontal members which assume the weight of concrete or masonry walls above door and window openings are called LINTELS.

TRUSSES

A beam of given strength, without intermediate supports below, can support a given load over only a certain maximum span. If the span is wider than this maximum, intermediate supports, such as a column must be provided for the beam. Sometimes it is not feasible or possible to install intermediate supports. When such is the case, a TRUSS may be used instead of a beam.

A beam consists of a single horizontal member. A truss, however, is a framework, consisting of two horizontal (or nearly horizontal) members, joined together by a number of vertical and/or inclined members. The horizontal members are called the UPPER and LOWER CHORDS; the vertical and/or inclined members are called the WEB MEMBERS.

ROOF MEMBERS

The horizontal or inclined members which provide support to a roof are called RAFTERS. The lengthwise (right angle to the rafters) member which support the peak ends of the rafters in a roof is called the RIDGE. (The ridge may be called the Ridge board, the Ridge PIECE, or the Ridge pole.) Lengthwise members other than ridges are called PURLINS. In wood frame construction the wall ends of rafters are supported on horizontal members called RAFTER PLATES, which are in turn supported by the outside wall studs. In concrete or masonry wall construction, the wall ends of rafters may be anchored directly on the walls, or on plates bolted to the walls.

II. CONSTRUCTION DRAWINGS

Construction drawings are drawings in which as much construction information as possible is presented GRAPHICALLY, or by means of pictures. Most construction drawings consist of ORTHOGRAPHIC views. GENERAL drawings consist of PLANS AND ELEVATIONS, drawn on a relatively small scale. DETAIL drawings consist of SECTIONS and DETAILS, drawn on a relatively large scale.

PLANS

A PLAN view is, as you know, a view of an object or area as it would appear if projected onto a horizontal plane passed through or held above the object or area. The most common construction plans are PLOT PLANS (also called SITE PLANS), FOUNDATION PLANS, FLOOR PLANS, and FRAMING PLANS.

A PLOT PLAN shows the contours, boundaries, roads, utilities, trees, structures, and any other significant physical features pertaining to or located on the site. The locations of proposed structures are indicated by appropriate outlines or floor plans. By locating the corners of a proposed structure at given distances from a REFERENCE or BASE line (which is shown on the plan and which can be located on the site), the plot plan provides essential data for those who will lay out the building lines. By indicating the elevations of existing and proposed earth surfaces (by means of CONTOUR lines), the plot plan provides essential data for the graders and excavators.

A FOUNDATION PLAN (fig. 3) is a plan view of a structure projected on a horizontal plane passed through (in imagination, of course) at the level of the tops of the foundations. The plan shown in figure 3 tells you that the main foundation of this structure will consist of a rectangular 12-in. concrete block wall, 22 ft

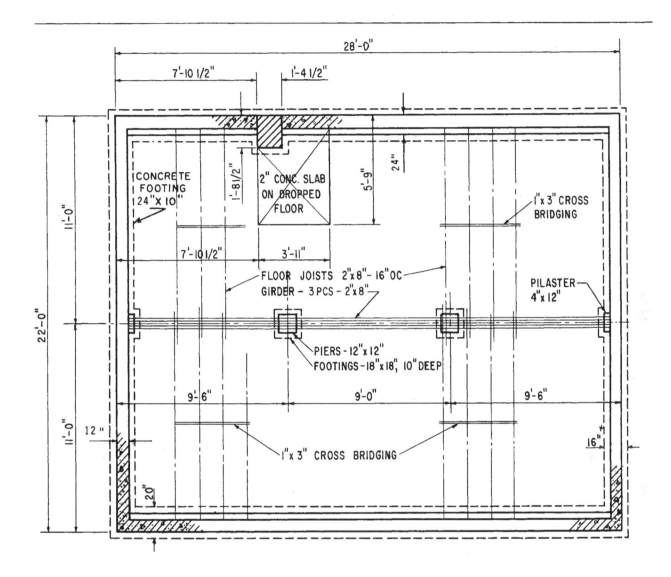

Figure 3.—Foundation plan.

wide by 28 ft long, centered on a concrete footing 24 in. wide. Besides the outside wall and footing, there will be two 12-in. square piers, centered on 18-in. square footings, and located on center 9 ft 6 in. from the end wall building lines. These piers will support a ground floor center-line girder.

A FLOOR PLAN (also called a BUILDING PLAN) is developed as shown in figure 4. Information on a floor plan includes the lengths, thicknesses, and character of the building walls at that particular floor, the widths and locations of door and window openings, the lengths and character of partitions, the number and arrangement of rooms, and the types and locations of utility installations. A typical floor plan is shown in figure 5.

FRAMING PLANS show the dimensions, numbers, and arrangement of structural members in wood frame construction. A simple FLOOR FRAMING PLAN is superimposed on the foundation plan shown in figure 3. From this foundation plan you learn that the ground-floor joists in this structure will consist of 2 x 8's, lapped at the girder, and spaced 16 in. O. C. The plan also shows that each row of joists is to be braced by a row of 1 x 3 cross bridging. For a more complicated floor framing problem, a framing plan like the one shown in figure 2-6 would be required. This plan

PERSPECTIVE VIEW OF A
BUILDING SHOWING CUTTING
PLANE WXY

PREVIOUS PERSPECTIVE VIEW AT
CUTTING PLANE WXYZ,
TOP REMOVED

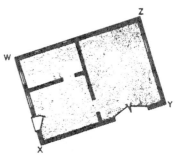

DEVELOPED FLOOR PLAN
WXYZ

Figure 4.—Floor plan development.

shows, among other things, the arrangement of joists and other members around stair wells and other floor openings.

A WALL FRAMING PLAN gives similar information with regard to the studs, corner posts, bracing, sills, plates, and other structural members in the walls. Since it is a view on a vertical plane, a wall framing plan is not a plan in the strict technical sense. However, the practice of calling it a plan has become a general custom. A ROOF FRAMING PLAN gives similar information with regard to the rafters, ridge, purlins, and other structural members in the roof.

A UTILITY PLAN is a floor plan which shows the layout of a heating, electrical, plumbing, or other utility system. Utility plans are used primarily by the ratings responsible for the utilities, but they are important to the Builder as well. Most utility installations require the leaving of openings in walls, floors, and roofs for the admission or installation of utility features. The Builder who is placing a concrete foundation wall must study the utility plans to determine the number, sizes, and locations of the openings he must leave for utilities.

Figure 7 shows a heating plan. Figure 8 shows an electrical plan.

ELEVATIONS

ELEVATIONS show the front, rear, and sides of a structure projected on vertical planes parallel to the planes of the sides. Front, rear, right side, and left side elevations of a small building are shown in figure 9.

As you can see, the elevations give you a number of important vertical dimensions, such as the perpendicular distance from the finish floor to the top of the rafter plate and from the finish floor to the tops of door and window finished openings. They also show the locations and characters of doors and windows. Dimensions of window sash and dimensions and character of lintels, however, are usually set forth in a WINDOW SCHEDULE.

A SECTION view is a view of a cross-section, developed as indicated in figure 10. By general custom, the term is confined to views of cross-sections cut by vertical planes. A floor plan or foundation plan, cut by a horizontal plane, is, technically speaking, a section view as well as a plan view, but it is seldom called a section.

The most important sections are the WALL sections. Figure 11 shows three wall sections for three alternate types of construction for the building shown in figures 3, 5, 7 and 8. The angled arrows marked "A" in figure 5 indicate the location of the cutting plane for the sections.

The wall sections are of primary importance to the supervisors of construction and to the craftsmen who will do the actual building. Take the first wall section, marked "masonry construction," for example. Starting at the bottom, you learn that the footing will be concrete, 2 ft wide and 10 in. high. The vertical distance of the bottom of the footing below FINISHED GRADE (level of the finished earth surface around the house) "varies"—meaning that it will depend on the soil-bearing capacity at the particular site. The foundation wall will consist of

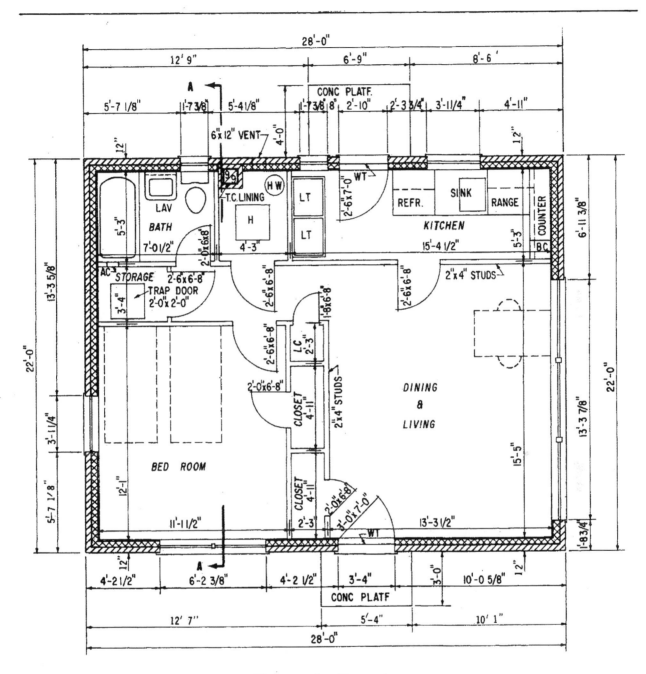

Figure 5.—Floor plan.

12-in. CMU, centered on the footing. Twelve-inch blocks will extend up to an unspecified distance below grade, where a 4-in. brick FACING (dimension indicated in the middle wall section) begins. Above the line of the bottom of the facing, it is obvious that 8-in. instead of 12-in. blocks will be used in the foundation wall.

The building wall above grade will consist of a 4-in. brick FACING TIER, backed by a BACKING TIER of 4-in. cinder blocks. The floor joists, consisting of 2 x 8's placed 16 in. O.C., will be anchored on 2 x 4 sills bolted to the top of the foundation wall. Every third joist will be additionally secured by a 2 x 1/4 STRAP ANCHOR embedded in the cinder block backing tier of the building wall.

The window (window B in the plan front elevation, fig. 9) will have a finished opening

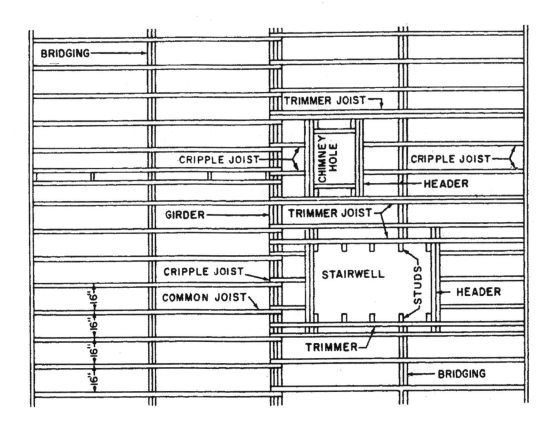

Figure 6.—Floor framing plan.

4 ft 2-5/8 in. high. The bottom of the opening will come 2 ft 11-3/4 in. above the line of the finished floor. As indicated in the wall section, (fig. 11) 13 masonry COURSES (layers of masonry units) above the finished floor line will amount to a vertical distance of 2 ft 11-3/4 in. As also indicated, another 19 courses will amount to the prescribed vertical dimension of the finished window opening.

Window framing details, including the placement and cross-sectional character of the lintel, are shown. The building wall will be carried 10-1/4 in., less the thickness of a 2 x 8 RAFTER PLATE, above the top of the window finished opening. The total vertical distance from the top of the finished floor to the top of the rafter plate will be 8 ft 2-1/4 in. Ceiling joists and rafters will consist of 2 x 6's, and the roof covering will consist of composition shingles laid on wood sheathing.

Flooring will consist of a wood finisher floor laid on a wood subfloor. Inside walls will be finished with plaster on lath (except on masonry wall which would be with or without lath as directed). A minimum of 2 vertical feet of crawl space will extend below the bottoms of the floor joists.

The middle wall section in figure 2-11 gives you similar information for a similar building constructed with wood frame walls and a DOUBLE-HUNG window. The third wall section shown in the figure gives you similar information for a similar building constructed with a steel frame, a casement window, and a concrete floor finished with asphalt tile.

DETAILS

DETAIL drawings are drawings which are done on a larger scale than that of the general drawings, and which show features not appearing at all, or appearing on too small a scale, on the general drawings. The wall sections just described are details as well as sections, since

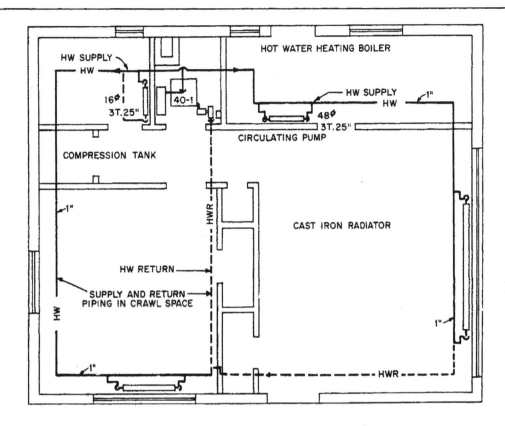

Figure 7.—Heating plan.

they are drawn on a considerable larger scale than the plans and elevations. Framing details at doors, windows, and cornices, which are the most common types of details, are practically always sections.

Details are included whenever the information given in the plans, elevations, and wall sections is not sufficiently "detailed" to guide the craftsmen on the job. Figure 12 shows some typical door and window wood framing details, and an eave detail for a very simple type of CORNICE. You should study these details closely to learn the terminology of framing members.

III.SPECIFICATIONS

The construction drawings contain much of the information about a structure which can be presented GRAPHICALLY (that is, in drawings). A very considerable amount of information can be presented this way, but there is more information which the construction supervisors and artisans must have and which is not adaptable to the graphic form of presentation. Information

of this kind includes quality criteria for materials (maximum amounts of aggregate per sack of cement, for example), specified standards of workmanship, prescribed construction methods, and the like.

Information of this kind is presented in a list of written SPECIFICATIONS, familiarly known as the "SPECS." A list of specifications usually begins with a section on GENERAL CONDITIONS. This section starts with a GENERAL DESCRIPTION of the building, including the type of foundation, type or types of windows, character of framing, utilities to be installed, and the like. Next comes a list of DEFINITIONS of terms used in the specs, and next certain routine declarations of responsibility and certain conditions to be maintained on the job.

SPECIFIC CONDITIONS are grouped in sections under headings which describe each of the major construction phases of the job. Separate specifications are written for each phase, and the phases are then combined to more or less follow the usual order of construction sequences on the job. A typical list of sections under "Specific Conditions" follows:

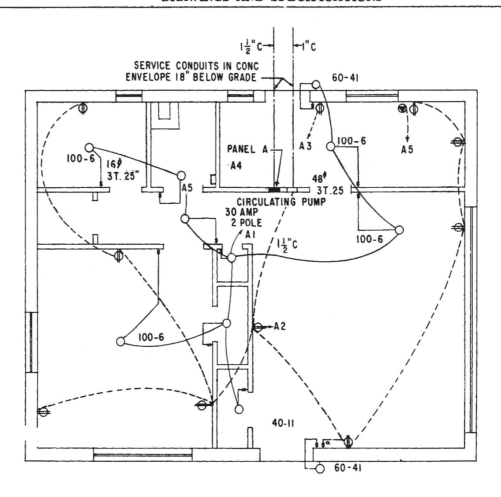

Figure   8.—Electrical plan.

2.—EARTHWORK 3.—CONCRETE 4.— MA-SONRY 5. — MISCELLANEOUS STEEL AND IRON 6. — CARPENTRY AND JOINERY 7.—LATHING AND PLASTERING 8.—TILE WORK 9. — FINISH FLOORING 10. — GLAZING 11.—FINISHING HARDWARE 12. — PLUMBING 13.—HEATING 14. — ELECTRICAL WORK 15.—FIELD PAINTING.

A section under "Specific Conditions" usually begins with a subsection of GENERAL RE-QUIREMENTS which apply to the phase of construction being considered. Under Section 6, CARPENTRY AND JOINERY, for example, the first section might go as follows:

6-01. GENERAL REQUIREMENTS. All framing, rough carpentry, and finishing woodwork required for the proper completion of the building shall be provided. All woodwork shall be protected from the weather, and the building shall be thoroughly dry before the finish is placed. All finish shall be dressed, smoothed, and sandpapered at the mill, and in addition shall be hand smoothed and sandpapered at the building where necessary to produce proper finish. . Nailing shall be done, as far as practicable, in concealed places, and all nails in finishing work shall be set. All lumber shall be S4S (meaning, "surfaced on 4 sides"); all materials for millwork and finish shall be kiln-dried; all rough and framing lumber shall be air- or kiln-dried. Any cutting, fitting, framing, and blocking necessary for the accommodation of other work shall be provided. All nails, spikes, screws, bolts, plates, clips, and other fastenings and rough hardware necessary for the proper completion of the building shall be provided.

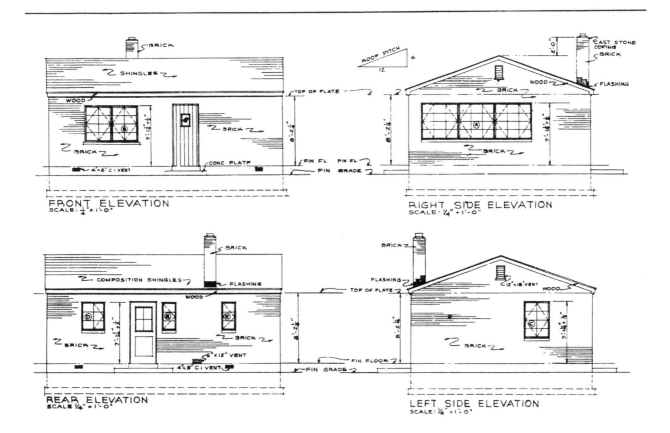

Figure 2-9.—Elevations.

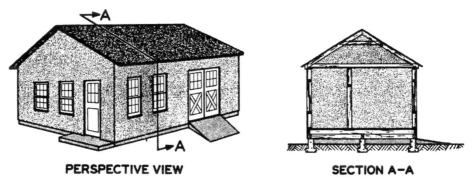

PERSPECTIVE VIEW

SECTION A-A

TYPICAL SMALL BUILDING SHOWING CUTTING PLANE A-A AND SECTION
DEVELOPED FROM THE CUTTING PLANE

Figure 10.—Development of a section view.

All finishing hardware shall be installed in accordance with the manufacturers' directions. Calking and flashing shall be provided where indicated, or where necessary to provide weathertight construction.

Next after the General Requirements for Carpentry and Joinery, there is generally a subsection on "Grading," in which the kinds and grades of the various woods to be used in the structure are specified. Subsequent subsections

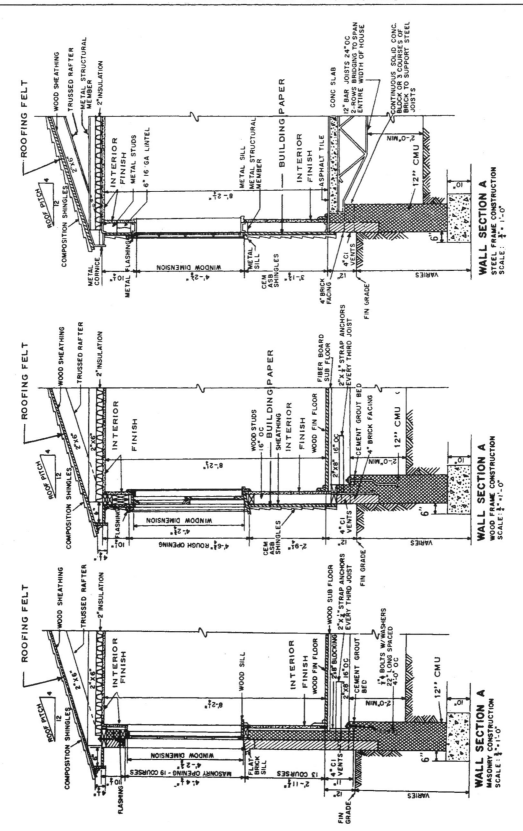

Figure 11.—Wall sections

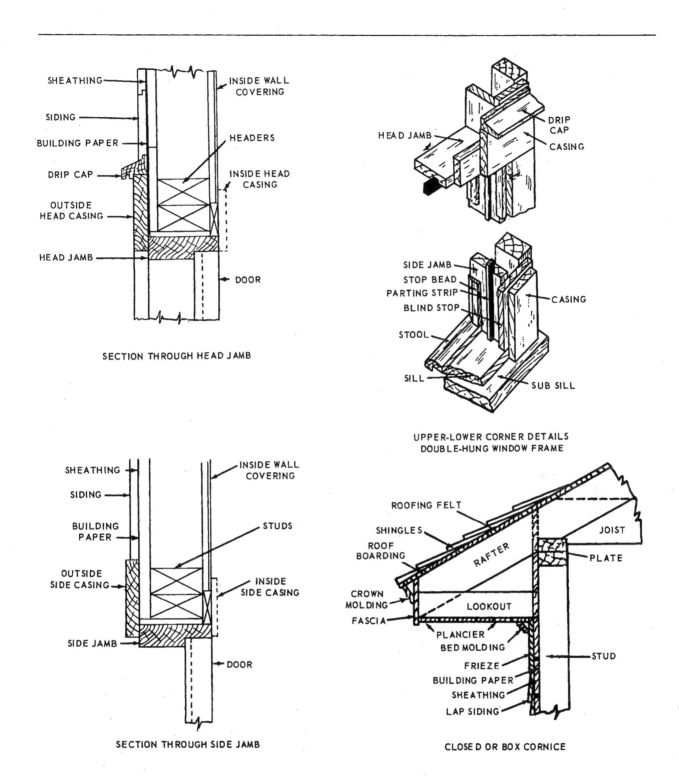

SECTION THROUGH HEAD JAMB

SHEATHING
SIDING
BUILDING PAPER
DRIP CAP
OUTSIDE HEAD CASING
HEAD JAMB
INSIDE WALL COVERING
HEADERS
INSIDE HEAD CASING
DOOR

SECTION THROUGH SIDE JAMB

SHEATHING
SIDING
BUILDING PAPER
OUTSIDE SIDE CASING
SIDE JAMB
INSIDE WALL COVERING
STUDS
INSIDE SIDE CASING
DOOR

HEAD JAMB
DRIP CAP
CASING

UPPER-LOWER CORNER DETAILS DOUBLE-HUNG WINDOW FRAME

SIDE JAMB
STOP BEAD
PARTING STRIP
BLIND STOP
STOOL
SILL
CASING
SUB SILL

CLOSED OR BOX CORNICE

ROOFING FELT
SHINGLES
ROOF BOARDING
CROWN MOLDING
FASCIA
PLANCIER
BED MOLDING
FRIEZE
BUILDING PAPER
SHEATHING
LAP SIDING
RAFTER
JOIST
PLATE
LOOKOUT
STUD

Figure   12.—Door, window and eave details.

specify various quality criteria and standards of workmanship for the various aspects of the rough and finish carpentry work, under such headings as FRAMING; SILLS, PLATES, AND GIRDERS; FLOOR JOISTS AND ROOF RAFTERS; STUDDING; and so on. An example of one of these subsections follows:

STUDDING for walls and partitions shall have doubled plates and doubled stud caps. Studs shall be set plumb and not to exceed 16-in. centers and in true alignment; they shall be bridged with one row of 2 x 4 pieces, set flatwise, fitted tightly, and nailed securely to each stud. Studding shall be doubled around openings and the heads of openings shall rest on the inner studs. Openings in partitions having widths of 4 ft and over shall be trussed. In wood frame construction, studs shall be trebled at corners to form posts.

From the above samples, you can see that a knowledge of the relevant specifications is as essential to the construction supervisor and the construction artisan as a knowledge of the construction drawings.

It is very important that the proper spec be used to cover the material requested. In cases in which the material is not covered by a Government spec, the ASTM (American Society for Testing Materials) spec or some other approved commercial spec may be used. It is EXTREMELY IMPORTANT in using specifications to cite all amendments, including the latest changes.

As a rule, the specs are provided for each project by the A/E (ARCHITECT-ENGINEERS). These are the OFFICIAL guidelines approved by the chief engineer or his representative for use during construction. These requirements should NOT be deviated from without prior approval from proper authority. This approval is usually obtained by means of a change order. When there is disagreement between the specifications and drawings, the specifications should normally be followed; however, check with higher authority in each case.

IV. BUILDER'S MATHEMATICS

The Builder has many occasions for the employment of the processes of ordinary arithmetic, and he must be thoroughly familiar with the methods of determining the areas and volumes of the various plane and solid geometrical figures. Only a few practical applications and a few practical suggestions, will be given here.

RATIO AND PROPORTION

There are a great many practical applications of ratio and proportion in the construction field. A few examples are as follows:

Some dimensions on construction drawings (such as, for example, distances from base lines and elevations of surfaces) are given in ENGINEER'S instead of CARPENTER's measure. Engineer's measure is measure in feet and decimal parts of a foot, or in inches and decimal parts of an inch, such as 100.15 ft or 11.14 in. Carpenter's measure is measure in yards, feet, inches, and even-denominator fractions of an inch, such as 1/2 in., 1/4 in., 1/16 in., 1/32 in., and 1/64 in.

You must know how to convert an engineer's measure given on a construction drawing to a carpenter's measure. Besides this, it will often happen that calculations you make yourself may produce a result in feet and decimal parts of a foot, which result you will have to convert to carpenter's measure. To convert engineer's to carpenter's measure you can use ratio and proportion as follows:

Let's say that you want to convert 100.14 ft to feet and inches to the nearest 1/16 in. The 100 you don't need to convert, since it is already in feet. What you need to do, first, is to find out how many twelfths of a foot (that is, how many inches) there are in 14/100 ft. Set this up as a proportional equation as follows: x:12::14:100.

You know that in a proportional equation the product of the means equals the product of the extremes. Consequently, 100x = (12 x 14), or 168. Then x = 168/100, or 1.68 in. Next question is, how many 16ths of an in. are there in 68/100 in.? Set this up, too, as a proportional equation, thus: x:16::68:100. Then 100x = 1088, and x = 10 88/100 sixteenths. Since 88/100 of a sixteenth is more than one-half of a sixteenth, you ROUND OFF by calling it 11/16. In 100.14 ft, then, there are 100 ft 1 11/16 in. For example:

A.
$$\underbrace{x:12::14:100}_{\text{Extremes}}$$

Product of extremes = product of means:

$$100 \ x = 168$$
$$x = 1.68 \text{ IN.}$$

B.   x:16::68:100

$$100 \ x = 1088$$

$$x = 10.88$$

$$x = 10 \ \frac{88}{100} \text{ sixteenths}$$

Rounded off to 11/16

Another way to convert engineer's measurements to carpenter's measurements is to multiply the decimal portion of a foot by 12 to get inches; multiply the decimal by 16 to get the fraction of an inch.

There are many other practical applications of ratio and proportion in the construction field. Suppose, for example, that a table tells you that, for the size and type of brick wall you happen to be laying, 12,321 bricks and 195 cu ft of mortar are required per every 1000 sq ft of wall. How many bricks and how much mortar will be needed for 750 sq ft of the same wall? You simply set up equations as follows; for example:

Brick: x:750::12,321:1000
Mortar: x:750::195:1000

Brick: $\dfrac{X}{750} = \dfrac{12,321}{1000}$ Cross multiply

$$1000 \ X = 9,240,750 \quad \text{Divide}$$
$$X = 9,240.75 = 9241 \text{ Brick.}$$

Mortar: $\dfrac{X}{750} = \dfrac{195}{1000}\cdot$ Cross multiply

$$1000 \ X = 146,250 \quad \text{Divide}$$
$$X = 146.25 = 146 \ 1/4 \text{ cu ft}$$

Suppose, for another example, that the ingredient proportions by volume for the type of concrete you are making are 1 cu ft cement to 1.7 cu ft sand to 2.8 cu ft coarse aggregate. Suppose you know as well, by reference to a table, that ingredients combined in the amounts indicated will produce 4.07 cu ft of concrete. How much of each ingredient will be required to make a cu yd of concrete?

Remember here, first, that there are not 9, but 27 (3 ft x 3 ft x 3 ft) cu ft in a cu yd. Your proportional equations will be as follows:

Cement: x:27::1:4.07

Sand: x:27::1.7:4.07

Coarse aggregate: x:27::2.8:4.07

Cement: x:27::1:4.07

$$\frac{x}{27} = \frac{1}{4.07}$$

$$4.07 \ x = 27$$

$$x = 6.63 \text{ cu ft Cement}$$

Sand: x:27::1.7:4.07

$$\frac{x}{27} = \frac{1.7}{4.07}$$

$$4.07 \ x = 45.9$$

$$x = 11.28 \text{ cu ft Sand}$$

Coarse aggregate: x:27::2.8:407

$$\frac{x}{27} = \frac{2.8}{4.07}$$

$$4.07 \ x = 75.6$$

$$x = 18.57 \text{ cu ft Coarse aggregate}$$

ARITHMETICAL OPERATIONS

The formulas for finding the area and volume of geometric figures are expressed in algebraic equations which are called formulas. A few of the more important formulas and their mathematical solutions will be discussed in this section.

To get an area, you multiply 2 linear measures together, and to get a volume you multiply 3 linear measures together. The linear measures you multiply together must all be expressed in the SAME UNITS; you cannot, for example, multiply a length in feet by a width in inches to get a result in square feet or in square inches.

Dimensions of a feature on a construction drawing are not always given in the same units. For a concrete wall, for example, the length and height are usually given in feet and the thickness in inches. Furthermore, you may want to get a result in units which are different from any shown on the drawing. Concrete volume, for example, is usually expressed in cubic yards, while the dimensions of concrete work are given on the drawings in feet and inches.

You can save yourself a good many steps in calculating by using fractions to convert the original dimension units into the desired end-result units. Take 1 in., for example. To express 1 in. in feet, you simply put it over 12, thus: 1/12 ft. To express 1 in. in yards, you simply put it over 36, thus: 1/36 yd. In the same manner, to express 1 ft in yards you simply put it over 3, thus 1/3 yd.

Suppose now that you want to calculate the number of cu yd of concrete in a wall 32 ft long by 14 ft high by 8 in. thick. You can express all these in yards and set up your problem thus:

$$\frac{32}{3} \times \frac{14}{3} \times \frac{8}{36}$$

Next you can cancel out, thus:

$$\frac{\overset{16}{\cancel{32}}}{3} \times \frac{\cancel{14}}{3} \times \frac{8}{\underset{\underset{9}{\cancel{18}}}{\cancel{36}}} = \frac{896}{81}$$

Dividing 896 by 81, you get 11.06 cu yds of concrete in the wall.

The right triangle is a triangle which contains one right (90°) angle. The following letters will denote the parts of the triangle indicated in figure 2-13—a = altitude, b = base, c = hypotenuse.

In solving a right triangle, the length of any side may be found if the lengths of the other two sides are given. The combinations of 3-4-5 (lengths of sides) or any multiple of these combinations will come out to a whole number. The following examples show the formula for finding

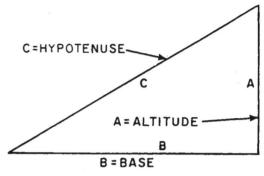

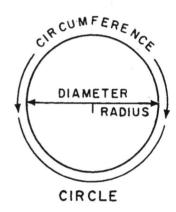

Figure 13.—Right triangle and circle.

each side. Each of these formulas is derived from the master formula $c^2 = a^2 + b^2$.

(1) Find c when a = 3, and b = 4.

$$c = \sqrt{a^2 + b^2} = \sqrt{3^2 + 4^2} = \sqrt{9 + 16} = \sqrt{25} = 5$$

(2) Find a when b = 8, and c = 10.

$$a = \sqrt{c^2 - b^2} = \sqrt{10^2 - 8^2} = \sqrt{100 - 64} = \sqrt{36} = 6$$

(3) Find b when a = 9, and c = 15.

$$b = \sqrt{c^2 - a^2} = \sqrt{15^2 - 9^2} = \sqrt{225 - 81} = \sqrt{144} = 12.$$

There are tables from which the square roots of numbers may be found; otherwise, they may be found arithmetically as explained later in this chapter.

Areas And Volumes Of Geometric Figures

This section on areas and volumes of geometric figures will be limited to the most commonly used geometric figures. Reference books, such as Mathematics, Vol. 1, are available for additional information if needed. Areas are expressed in square units and volumes in cubic units.

1. A circle is a plane figure bounded by a curved line every point of which is the same distance from the center.
   a. The curved line is called the circumference.
   b. A straight line drawn from the center to any point on the circumference is called a radius. (r = 1/2 the diameter.)
   c. A straight line drawn from one point of the circumference through the center and terminating on the opposite point of the circumference is called a diameter. (d = 2 times the radius.) See figure 2-13.
   d. The area of a circle is found by the following formulas: $A = \pi r^2$ or $A = .7854\ d^2$. (π is pronounced pie = 3.1416 or 3 1/7, .7854 is 1/4 of π.) Example: Find the area of a circle whose radius is 7". $A = \pi r^2 = 3\ 1/7 \times 7^2 = 22/7 \times 49 = 154$ sq in. If you use the second formula you obtain the same results.
   e. The circumference of a circle is found by multiplying π times the diameter or 2 times π times the radius. Example: Find the circumference of a circle whose diameter is 56 inches. $C = \pi d = 3.1415 \times 56 = 175.9296$ inches.

2. The area of a right triangle is equal to one-half the product of the base by the altitude. (Area = 1/2 base x altitude.) Example: Find the area of a triangle whose base is 16" and altitude 6". Solution:

$$A = 1/2\ bh = 1/2 \times 16 \times 6 = 48 \text{ sq in.}$$

3. The volume of a cylinder is found by multiplying the area of the base times the height. ($V = 3.1416 \times r^2 \times h$). Example: Find the volume of a cylinder which has a radius of 8 in. and a height of 4 ft. Solution:

$$8 \text{ in} = \frac{2}{3} \text{ ft and } \left(\frac{2}{3}\right)2 = \frac{4}{9} \text{ sq ft.}$$

$$V = 3.1416 \times \frac{4}{9} \times 4 = \frac{50.2656}{9} = 5.59 \text{ cu ft.}$$

4. The volume of a rectangular solid equals the length x width x height. (V = lwh.) Example: Find the volume of a rectangular solid which has a length of 6 ft, a width of 3 ft, and a height of 2 ft. Solution:

$$V = lwh = 6 \times 3 \times 2 = 36 \text{ cu ft.}$$

5. The volume of a cone may be found by multiplying one-third times the area of the base times the height.

$$\left(V = \frac{1}{3} \pi r^2 h\right)$$

Example: Find the volume of a cone when the radius of its base is 2 ft and its height is 9 ft. Solution:

$$\pi = 3.1416, r = 2, 2^2 = 4$$

$$V = \frac{1}{3} r^2 h = \frac{1}{3} \times 3.1416 \times 4 \times 9 = 37.70 \text{ cu ft.}$$

Powers And Roots

1. Powers—When we multiply several numbers together, as 2 x 3 x 4 = 24, the numbers 2, 3, and 4 are factors and 24 the product. The operation of raising a number to a power is a special case of multiplication in which the factors are all equal. The power of a number is the number of times the number itself is to be taken as a factor. Example: 2^4 is 16. The second power is called the square of the number, as 3^2. The third power of a number is called the cube of the number, as 5^3. The exponent of a number is a number placed to the right and above a base to show how many times the base is used as a factor. Example:

$$4^3 \longleftarrow \text{ exponent} = $$
$$\text{base}$$

$$4 \times 4 \times 4 = 64.$$

2. Roots—To indicate a root, use the sign $\sqrt{\ }$, which is called the radical sign. A small figure, called the index of the root, is placed in the opening of the sign to show which root is to be taken. The square root of a number is one of the two equal factors into which a number is

divided. Example: $\sqrt{81} = \sqrt{9 \times 9} = 9$. The cube root is one of the three equal factors into which a number is divided. Example: $\sqrt[3]{125} = \sqrt[3]{5 \times 5 \times 5} = 5$.

Square Root

1. The square root of any number is that number which, when multiplied by itself, will produce the first number. For example; the square root of 121 is 11 because 11 times 11 equals 121.

2. How to extract the square root arithmetically:

$$\begin{array}{r} 95. \\ \sqrt{9025} \quad \sqrt{90'25.} \end{array}$$

$$\begin{array}{r} : -81 \\ 180 : \quad 925 \\ +5 : \quad -925 \\ \hline 185 : \quad 000 \end{array}$$

a. Begin at the decimal point and divide the given number into groups of 2 digits each (as far as possible), going from right to left and/or left to right.

b. Find the greatest number (9) whose square is contained in the first or left hand group (90). Square this number (9) and place it under the first pair of digits (90), then subtract.

c. Bring down the next pair of digits (25) and add it to the remainder (9).

d. Multiply the first digit in the root by 20 and use it as a trial divisor (180). This trial divisor (180) will go into the new dividend (925) five times. This number, 5 (second digit in the root), is added back to the trial divisor, obtaining the true divisor (185).

e. The true divisor (185) is multiplied by the second digit (5) and placed under the remainder (925). Subtract and the problem is solved.

f. If there is still a remainder and you want to carry the problem further, add zeros (in pairs) and continue the above process.

Coverage Calculations

You will frequently have occasion to estimate the number of linear feet of boards of a given size, or the number of tiles, asbestos shingles, and the like, required to cover a given area. Let's take the matter of linear feet of boards first.

What you do here is calculate, first, the number of linear feet of board required to cover 1 sq ft. For boards laid edge-to-edge, you base your calculations on the total width of a board. For boards which will lap each other, you base your calculations on the width laid TO THE WEATHER, meaning the total width minus the width of the lap.

Since there are 144 sq in. in a sq ft, linear footage to cover a given area can be calculated as follows. Suppose your boards are to be laid 8 in. to the weather. If you divide 8 in. into 144 sq in., the result (which is 18 in., or 1.5 ft) will be the linear footage required to cover a sq ft. If you have, say, 100 sq ft to cover, the linear footage required will be 100 x 1.5, or 150 ft.

To estimate the number of tiles, asbestos shingles, and the like required to cover a given area, you first calculate the number of units required to cover a sq ft. Suppose, for example, you are dealing with 9 in. x 9 in. asphalt tiles. The area of one of these is 9 in. x 9 in. or 81 sq in. In a sq ft there are 144 sq in. If it takes 1 to cover 81 sq in., how many will it take to cover 144 sq in.? Just set up a proportional equation, as follows.

$$1:81::x:144$$

When you work this out, you will find that it takes 1.77 tiles to cover a sq ft. To find the number of tiles required to cover 100 sq ft, simply multiply by 100. How do you multiply anything by 100? Just move the decimal point 2 places to the right. Consequently, it takes 177 9 x 9 asphalt tiles to cover 100 sq ft of area.

Board Measure

BOARD MEASURE is a method of measuring lumber in which the basic unit is an abstract volume 1 ft long by 1 ft wide by 1 in. thick. This abstract volume or unit is called a BOARD FOOT.

There are several formulas for calculating the number of board feet in a piece of given dimensions. Since lumber dimensions are most frequently indicated by width and thickness in inches and length in feet, the following formula is probably the most practical.

$$\frac{\text{Thickness in in. x width in in. x length in ft}}{12}$$

= board feet

Suppose you are calculating the number of board feet in a 14-ft length of 2 x 4. Applying the formula, you get:

$$\frac{\overset{1}{\cancel{2}} \times \overset{2}{\cancel{4}} \times 14}{\underset{\underset{3}{\cancel{6}}}{\cancel{12}}} = \frac{28}{3} = 9 \ 1/3 \ \text{bd ft}$$

The chief practical use of board measure is in cost calculations, since lumber is bought and sold by the board foot. Any lumber less than 1 in. thick is presumed to be 1 in. thick for board measure purposes. Board measure is calculated on the basis of the NOMINAL, not the ACTUAL, dimensions of lumber.

The actual size of a piece of dimension lumber (such as a 2 x 4, for example) is usually less than the nominal size.